The FLAVOR of FRANCE

The FLAVOUR *of* FRANCE

in Recipes and Pictures

By NARCISSA G. CHAMBERLAIN

and NARCISSE CHAMBERLAIN

Photographs by Samuel Chamberlain

THE COOKERY BOOK CLUB
LONDON

Introduction

❧

The association of the landscapes of France with her cooking is irresistible, as any traveler in that remarkable country remembers. The returned tourist is as likely to refer to a French cathedral town as "the one where we had that marvellous *pâté en croûte*" as to quote its proper name. This may lead his friends to ask if he went to France to see the country or only to please his palate, and the answer is, of course, that in France it is not possible to do one without the other. It can even reasonably be maintained in the defense of good eating that there are innumerable cultural meccas the sightseer might never have been exposed to, had he not incidentally known there was a top-notch restaurant on the way.

A day's motoring through the tempting French countryside is inevitably punctuated by a meal with the overtones of a feast, even if it is only a picnic gathered together from the pushcarts of a village market or lunch in an anonymous bistro. In the provinces the occasion may produce regional specialties as characteristic of their native areas as the roof lines of the local architecture. And occasionally one must indulge in a feast in earnest at a gastronomic shrine. In each case, like wine in a sauce, the setting is a tangible ingredient of memorable meals in France.

So a profile of France in pictures seems the most logical embellishment a collection of her recipes could have. They appear in this book to add a little of the flavor of France herself to the reconstruction of some of those memorable meals.

But there is a subtle difficulty in bringing to life in one's own kitchen the delectable memories of gastronomic travels or the temptations of French recipe books. Most of us do not wish to eat at home as we do in restaurants, nor would we want to cook like expert chefs every day, even if we knew how. There is something missing in the average epicure's experience of French food. Ironically, the missing link is the most common cuisine of the country, *la cuisine bourgeoise,* made up of the day-to-day offerings of the good *cuisinière,* or family cook. So the authors do not apologize for presenting here many recipes that are standard old favorites. These are the dishes that win new friends and influence new cooks and keep a firm hold on those who no longer need to be persuaded that there is nothing in the world quite like a good French meal.

We were once upon a time blessed by the presence of a *cuisinière* in our own kitchen and that is perhaps the only way to discover just exactly what the philosophy of French food in every-day life really is. (Philosophy seems to us only slightly too large a word for it.) It consists first of a touch of perfectionism. In the *cuisinière*'s modest repertory, this ingredient gives results out of all proportion to the work involved. Then there is a series of traditional recipes which happen to be the very roots of *haute cuisine* but which have an unshakable modesty that sets them apart from it. Next comes that ubiquitous charmer, the bottle of wine, often a very humble article indeed, which Anglo-Saxon civilization is finally learning to accept with the proper calm. And lastly, there is a surprising simplicity of menu.

French people themselves tend to conceal this civilized formula from their foreign guests, much as their restaurants do also. The menus they offer visitors to their homes are totally different from those that are served *en famille.* Tradition and good manners require on these occasions that the *cuisinière* produce a meal worthy of a chef, and it is a credit to the every-day cooks of France that they can so often do it. Their more elaborate repertory may be brief, but it is impeccable.

It is perfectly possible, though you shouldn't let it happen, to travel all through France and never eat a *blanquette de veau.* Your French friends will not think it correct to serve this homely treasure to you and, unless you know how to seek out the quiet bourgeois eating places well off the beaten track, you will not find it on a restaurant menu. That famous classic, *boeuf bourguignon,* is more common in the French restaurants of New York City than it is in those of Paris. If you have chicken in a French household, it will not be the *poule au riz* with which the family is regaled when there are no guests to be honored. In short, there seems to be a sort of polite conspiracy afoot to obscure one of the most delightful, and certainly most useful, aspects of French cooking: the famous French sense of *mesure*—that common sense which Frenchmen so patently do not apply to their politics and which they do apply to the average day's lunch and dinner.

We have tried in this small book to demonstrate the approachability of French kitchen tradition and to provide some gastronomic glamour as well, in thoroughly practical form. The recipes are not all of equal simplicity, for the cook must have her fund of specialties for festive occasions, but they are designed for sensible cooks, not expert chefs, and they are presented in familiar American kitchen language and measurements.

On page xv is a list of some of the French cook's old stand-bys, a number of them main dishes around which a down-to-earth family meal is constructed, often with nothing more elaborate to complete it than the well-known triumvirate of salad, cheese and fruit. A sampling of regional specialties appears on page xvi. A good number of these are as familiar all over France as they are in their native provinces and they are household recipes.

In the back of the book is a group of menus which are as French and as traditional as we could make them. They must be approached, however, with *mesure,* since some of them are intended for entertaining, for grand occasions, or are perhaps just to dream about. But many of them are the tidy little pieces of perfection for every day which seem to us most nostalgic and delightful of all. Most simple French dishes require a little extra attention to detail; the secret of the ideal little French menu is that it leaves time (and appetite) for this extra something that makes all the difference.

To take care of every eventuality, a number of our menus are full-scale dinners. These may not always suit your purposes; if not, we hope you will simply cut them down rather than dismiss them as "too much." Finally, various categories of dishes, from hors-d'oeuvre and soups through desserts and pastries, can be located through the menu planner on page 221. From these we hope you will be tempted to create French menus of your own, for our brief group is meant primarily as a guide to planning others.

In adapting French menus to American customs, one course that can be perplexing is the hors-d'oeuvre. Cold hors-d'oeuvre, particularly the *hors-d'oeuvre variés* listed on page 217, are served only at the midday meal, which in France is also the main meal of the day. These should not appear in our American evening dinner. But there are other possibilities, and it depends on your point of view whether or not you find hors-d'oeuvre, hot or cold, plain or fancy, worth the trouble. Certainly one natural way to simplify a meal is to eliminate them, as we have indicated with parentheses in some of our menus. But hors-d'oeuvre are a refinement ingrained in the French way of life. They have become simpler of recent decades, but not casually expendable.

They were once quite a bone of contention with a young American friend of ours who married a Frenchman and are referred to in her household as *un petit quelque chose pour commencer.* Back in the days when she was a young bride doing battle with her first *boeuf à la mode,* her husband's adamant request for his "little something to start with" in addition strained her good nature severely. It would never enter a Frenchman's head, however, to clutter up his wife's hard-working day with demands for the cakes, pies and cookies that are produced in quantities in some American households. So, as far as hard labor in the kitchen is concerned, there may turn out to be less of it the French way. But the real point is that you can easily become addicted to hors-d'oeuvre, for they civilize a meal as no single other thing can do.

Except, of course, wine. The first law of wine-drinking is that neither the wine nor the meal are at their best without the other. The second law is that the wine must be appropriate to the occasion. The question of what is appropriate can become exquisitely complicated; it starts, however, with simple common sense. An ordinary meal calls for a *vin ordinaire;* better wines are for more elaborate dishes. This charming dialogue can reach exalted heights if you are either an expert or a millionaire, and preferably both. If you are an American, there is a third law which says that many of our domestic wines are as good as any *vin ordinaire,* that others are noticeably better than inferior French imports, and that still others are positively excellent. Our menus therefore list American alternatives to French wines wherever possible.

There is also the problem of when to serve a red or a white wine. The basic rule, of course, is red wine with meat and white with fish, but this does not cover all the possibilities, by any means. In brief, the usual combinations are: with all fish and sea food, a dry white wine; with red meat, game, duck and goose, a red wine; with chicken, turkey, veal, pork and ham, either a light red or a dry white wine; with cheese, red wine—and if you are having a dinner with several wines, serve the best one of all with the cheese, for all wines, as a rule, show up at their best with it; with desserts, a sweet white wine such as a Bordeaux, or a dry champagne (needless to say, this is not a daily practice).

Rosé wines are popular in France, as they are in America, though the purists take a dim view of them. There are only a few aristocrats, such as Tavel, among them. But of a hot summer's day a simple *vin rosé,* served chilled, with meat, fish or fowl, is a delight and a wise choice as well, for it can take the place of a heavier red wine that is not at its best in warm weather.

For very festive menus, the serving of champagne throughout the meal is an accepted tradition, though the dedicated gourmet is inclined to disagree. He prefers an appropriate wine with each course; the champagne can wait until the dessert and the toasts.

The rules for serving temperatures of wine are simple: white and *rosé* wines, chilled but never icy; champagne, well iced; red wines, room temperature or just a bit below; sweet white wines, well chilled.

Wine, of course, is also a staple of French cooking itself. It is true that "cooking wine" should be as good as any wine you would drink, but don't pour a magnificent bottle of old Burgundy into a stew unless there is plenty more where the first one came from. Something infinitely more modest will really do very well. There are other staples of French cooking that are not usual in standard American fare. Herbs by now are standard, but shallots remain inexplicably hard to find and can be replaced by small white onions. The *bouquet garni* so often called for is usually composed of fresh parsley, thyme (dried or fresh), a piece of celery with its leaves, and a bay leaf. The customary assortment of *fines herbes,* always fresh, is parsley, chives, tarragon and chervil, all finely minced; the combination is varied according to what is available, however. *Fines herbes* turn up in many recipes, though their most familiar place is in omelettes and salads.

Stock, either chicken or beef, is a constant requirement. It is no longer realistic, though we wish it were, to expect every kitchen to be equipped with homemade stock at all times. Canned clear chicken broth is common in any market and usually excellent, but a word of warning about beef broths and consommés. There seem to be practically none available that do not have caramel color added. Their sweetened flavor absolutely rules them out for any recipe calling for beef stock; bouillon cubes or meat extract dissolved in boiling water will always be better.

We have been very cautious about including the more difficult recipes or those calling for ingredients that are not common in this country, so a number of your favorites may be missing. Our profile of France and her recipes is an abbreviated one which tells only a fraction of all that might be said. Though several encyclopedias and volumes numbering in the thousands have been filled by others on the subject, we hope our modest vignette will nevertheless make new friends for *la cuisine française* as well as please those who are already devoted to it.

NARCISSE CHAMBERLAIN

The FRENCH
PROVINCES

Contents

❦

List of Illustrations

Classics of the Family Kitchen

xv

Regional Specialties

THE EIFFEL TOWER AND THE STATUE OF MARSHAL JOFFRE *Paris*

French Vanilla Ice Cream
Glace Vanille
(Milk, vanilla bean, egg yolks, sugar, cream)

Scald 2 cups of milk in a saucepan. Turn off the flame and steep a vanilla bean in the milk for 20 minutes. Beat 6 egg yolks in the top of a double boiler until they are thick and lemon colored. Stir in ½ cup of granulated sugar, then slowly add the warm milk. Cook the mixture over barely simmering, never boiling, water, stirring constantly for about 7 minutes, or until it just coats the spoon. Remove the top of the double boiler immediately, set it in cold water to cool the custard, and stir in 2 cups of heavy cream.

This ice cream should, of course, be made in a hand freezer. However, if it *must* be done in the refrigerator, turn the controls to "very cold" and put the custard in a deep ice tray in the freezing compartment until it reaches the mushy stage. Then spoon it into a chilled bowl and beat it hard with an egg beater. Return it to the tray, freeze it some more, beat it again, then leave it to freeze solid for at least 3 hours, covered with wax paper to keep crystals from forming on top. Makes 3 pints.

1

FOUNTAIN OF NEPTUNE, PLACE STANISLAS—NANCY   *Lorraine*

Hot Lorraine Tart
Quiche Lorraine
(Pastry, ham, onion, eggs, milk, spices)

Line a 10-inch pie pan with a thin layer of your favorite pastry dough. Over this scatter ⅓ cup of finely diced ham. Slice 2 onions, sauté them gently in butter until they are soft but not brown, and spread them over the ham. Beat 4 eggs with a pinch of salt, a little grated nutmeg and a few grains of cayenne pepper. Very gradually stir 2 cups of hot milk into the eggs. Heat the mixture slowly over a low fire and stir it until it just begins to thicken. Pour this custard carefully into the pie shell. Bake the *quiche* in a 375° oven for about ½ hour or until it is set and golden on top. Serve hot, directly from the pan.

VILLAGE IN THE MIDI *Provence*

Noëlie's Eggplant Toulouse

Aubergine Toulousaine à la Noëlie

(Eggplant, oil, garlic, parsley, croutons, tomato sauce)

Peel and slice an eggplant, salt the slices and let them stand under pressure for ½ hour. Drain and dry the slices. Dip them in flour and brown them on both sides in hot oil almost ½ inch deep in the pan. The eggplant will absorb the oil very fast. Put the eggplant on a hot platter and keep it warm. Chop finely 1 clove of garlic and 2 or 3 sprigs of parsley and heat them in the remaining oil; be careful not to burn them and add more oil if necessary. Add ¾ cup of bread cut in small dice and brown it lightly. The bread will absorb the oil and turn into crisp, garlic-flavored croutons. Sprinkle them over the slices of eggplant and serve with tomato sauce.

THE YACHT BASIN—MONTE CARLO *Riviera*

Stewed White Beans from Southern France

Haricots Blancs à la Moustierenco

(Dried white beans, herbs, onion, olive oil, tomato, meat juice, garlic)

Soak 2 cups of dried white beans overnight in water to cover. Drain them, cover them with boiling salted water, and add a *bouquet garni,* 1 stalk of celery with its leaves, and 1 small onion stuck with a clove. Cook the beans slowly until they are tender but still firm; drain them and remove the onion, celery and herbs. In a skillet sauté 1 medium onion, chopped, in 1 tablespoon of olive oil until it is golden. Add 1 large tomato, peeled, seeded and chopped, and simmer together for 4 or 5 minutes. Add a little brown juice from a roast, or 1 teaspoon of meat glaze dissolved in ¼ cup of the water in which the beans were cooked. Then add the beans, cover, and simmer them for 20 minutes. A few minutes before serving, taste for seasoning and add a very finely minced half clove of garlic. The beans should be very tender but not mushy. Serves six.

4

THE LAC D'ANNECY AT TALLOIRES *Savoy*

Creamed Water Cress Soup

Velouté Cressonière

(Potatoes, water cress, cream, egg yolks, butter)

Peel and slice 1 pound of potatoes. Cut off about 3 dozen perfect leaves from a large bunch of water cress and put them aside. Chop the rest of the water cress coarsely and sauté it in a soup kettle in 1 tablespoon of butter until it is somewhat softened. Add 5 to 6 cups of salted boiling water and the sliced potatoes, and simmer all together for 20 minutes, or until the potatoes are soft. Pour the soup through a sieve into a saucepan and force through as much as possible of the vegetables. Bring the soup back to the boil, add the reserved water cress leaves, and simmer it another 2 or 3 minutes only.

In a small bowl mix together ¼ cup of heavy cream and 2 egg yolks and stir in a few spoonfuls of the hot soup. Take the soup off the fire and slowly stir in the egg and cream mixture. Add a lump of butter, taste the *velouté* for seasoning, and reheat it briefly without letting it boil. Serve immediately. Serves six.

REMNANTS OF A MEDIEVAL TOWN—TRÈVES *Anjou*

Curried Chicken in Cream

Fondue de Poulet à l'Indienne

(Chicken, onion, curry powder, brandy, cream)

French cooks use curry only to flavor a sauce, not to make it exotically hot or spicy. A curried dish is nevertheless poetically named *à l'indienne*.

Cut a roasting chicken into pieces as for a fricassee. In a heavy skillet brown the pieces on all sides in 4 tablespoons of butter. Add 1 minced onion, 1 cup of chicken stock, cover the skillet and simmer the chicken gently until it is tender. Then pour in a liqueur glass of warmed brandy and set it aflame, shaking the pan back and forth until the flame dies. Remove the chicken to a serving dish and keep it warm. Add 1½ cups of heavy cream and 1 teaspoon of curry powder to the pan juices and simmer the sauce until it is slightly reduced. Work 1 teaspoon of butter to a smooth paste with 1 teaspoon flour and blend this into the sauce. Strain the sauce through a fine sieve and pour it over the chicken.

6

HAMLET IN THE FOOTHILLS—ASPERS-SUR-BUECH *Dauphiny*

Strawberry Tart

Tarte aux Fraises

(Pastry, strawberries, raspberry jelly)

Use your favorite pastry recipe for this *tarte aux fraises*. Line a pie plate (or a straight-sided tart ring) with a thin layer of the pastry dough and press a circle of waxed paper over it to keep it flat as it bakes. Bake the pastry shell for ¼ hour in a 450° oven. Cool the shell and fill it with neat rows of raw, hulled strawberries, stem ends down. Stir 1 cup of raspberry jelly thoroughly with 2 tablespoons of water and spoon it over the strawberries. Heat the tart for 5 minutes in a hot oven just before serving.

SUNDAY MORNING IN CLAMECY *Nivernais*

Ham in Cream Nivernaise

Jambon à la Crème Nivernaise

(Ham, unsalted butter, white wine, chicken consommé, cream)

In a heavy skillet heat 8 slices of cooked ham in 2 tablespoons of unsalted butter. Cook the ham on both sides but do not let it brown. Add 1 cup of dry white wine and let the liquid in the pan reduce to a very small quantity. Put the slices of ham on a warm platter and keep it hot. Blend a teaspoon of flour into the pan juices, stir in 1 cup of chicken consommé and simmer the sauce for about 5 minutes. Then add ½ cup of heavy cream and pour the sauce over the ham. Serves four.

8

PLACE DE LA CONCORDE   *Paris*

Filets of Beef Béarnaise

Tournedos Béarnaise

(Beef tenderloin, croutons, and a sauce of egg yolks, cream, butter, vinegar, herbs)

Brown 4 1-inch-thick slices of beef tenderloin on each side in a little butter, leaving the meat rare in the center. Meanwhile trim 4 slices of bread to fit the size and shape of the tenderloins. Sauté these croutons in butter until they are golden brown and crisp, and put one under each tenderloin.

Serve with the following luxurious *sauce béarnaise:* In a small earthenware bowl mix 2 egg yolks with 2 tablespoons of heavy cream, ¼ teaspoon of salt, a pinch of cayenne pepper and 1 tablespoon of tarragon vinegar. Fit the bowl into the top of a small pan of barely simmering water and stir the sauce with a wire whisk until it begins to thicken. Bit by bit add 4 tablespoons of butter, still stirring constantly. When the butter is melted and the sauce has become fairly thick, add 1 teaspoon of chopped tarragon and ½ teaspoon each of chopped parsley and chives. Serves four.

B   9

THE STEEP VALLEY   *Auvergne*

Braised Carrots

Carottes Vichy

(Carrots, butter, sugar)

Scrape a bunch of young carrots and slice them paper-thin. Cook them over a very low flame in a heavy pan, tightly covered, with ¼ cup of water, a pinch of salt, 1 teaspoon of sugar and a good lump of butter. In about 20 minutes the water should be completely evaporated and the carrots should be cooked and just beginning to glaze. Sprinkle them with chopped parsley before serving.

CASTLE ON A CLIFF—BEYNAC-ET-CAZENAC   *Périgord*

Creamed Ham Omelette

Omelette au Jambon à la Crème

(Eggs, ham, nutmeg, cream)

Heat 3 tablespoons of chopped ham in 1 tablespoon of butter and season it with a little nutmeg and freshly ground pepper. Blend in a scant teaspoon of flour, add 4 tablespoons of cream and stir the mixture until it is hot and slightly thickened. Spread the *jambon à la crème* across the center of a 4- or 6-egg omelette just before it is folded.

11

VINEYARDS AT BERÈZE-LA-VILLE

Burgundy

Veal Stew with Red Wine

Etuvée de Veau au Vin Rouge

(Veal, red wine, garlic, herbs)

Cut 1½ pounds of young veal into 1-inch cubes. Brown the veal in a heavy casserole in 2 tablespoons of butter. Add 1½ cups of red wine, ½ cup of water, salt and pepper, 2 whole cloves of garlic, parsley, and 1 bay leaf. Cover the casserole and simmer the veal for about 2 hours, adding more liquid if the sauce reduces too fast. Dissolve 1 tablespoon of flour in a little water or red wine, add it to the sauce, and cook the *étuvée* about ½ hour longer. Serves four.

QUAI DES ÉTATS-UNIS—NICE *Riviera*

Lamb Chops Niçoise

Côtelettes d'Agneau à la Niçoise

(Lamb chops, green beans, potatoes, tomatoes, white wine, garlic, tomato paste)

The mark of a dish from the Riviera is its gentle Mediterranean aroma of garlic, olive oil and ripe tomatoes. This particular recipe requires a modest effort in presentation.

Pan-broil 8 small rib lamb chops in 2 tablespoons of olive oil. Arrange them in the center of a hot platter. Around the chops arrange neat, alternating piles of buttered young green beans and small new potatoes browned in butter, and 8 tiny whole tomatoes sautéed in oil until partly softened.

To the juices in the pan in which the chops were cooked add 1 small chopped and mashed clove of garlic, 2 or 3 tablespoons of white wine, the same amount of veal or chicken stock, 1 teaspoon of tomato paste and ½ teaspoon of chopped tarragon. Heat the sauce, stirring briskly, and pour it over the chops. Serves four.

13

CHÂTEAU À LA FRANÇAISE—VAUX-LE-VICOMTE   *Ile-de-France*

Broiled Calf's Liver à la Française
Foie de Veau Grillé
(Calf's liver, garlic, tarragon vinegar, herbs)

The secret of good calf's liver is, above all, to use only young, tender liver that is very light in color. Secondly, liver must never be overcooked. Have your butcher slice it not too thin. Cook it only briefly, in hot butter, over a brisk fire; 2 minutes on each side should be plenty. The slices should be pale pink in the center and very tender. When the liver is almost cooked, add for each slice ½ finely chopped and mashed clove of garlic. Arrange the liver on a hot platter. For each slice stir 1 teaspoon of tarragon wine vinegar into the pan juices and add a little butter if the pan is dry. Pour this sauce over the liver. A dusting of finely chopped parsley is the indispensable last touch. If you have fresh tarragon to sprinkle on too, so much the better.

14

PREHISTORIC MENHIRS—CARNAC   *Brittany*

Breton Roast Lamb with White Beans
Gigot à la Bretonne
(Leg of lamb, garlic, white beans, tomato, onion)

A roast of lamb is unthinkable in provincial France without stewed white beans (*haricots*) to go with it. The Bretons perfect the combination by serving the *gigot* on a large, deep platter with the beans, which can then soak up every drop of the juice as the roast is carved. When planning this dish, first put 2 cups of dried white beans to soak in cold water overnight.

Cut 2 cloves of garlic in half lengthwise and insert the pieces near the bone at each end of a leg of young lamb. Remove as much skin and fat as possible from the roast, spread it with butter, give it a light dusting of freshly ground pepper, and roast it until it is done but still somewhat pink and juicy in the center.

Meanwhile drain the water from the beans and cover them with boiling salted water, add 2 whole peeled onions and a *bouquet garni*. Cook the beans slowly and drain them when they are tender but still firm. In another saucepan melt a generous lump of butter, add the 2 onions from the bean pot and 2 peeled, ripe tomatoes. Cook this mixture down to a purée, stir in the beans carefully so as not to break them, add a little juice from the roasting pan and simmer the *haricots* just long enough to heat them. Serves six.

CHÂTEAU DE TOUFFOU NEAR POITIERS   *Poitou*

Veal Chops Poitou

Côtes de Veau Poitou

(Veal chops, shallots, bacon, stock, white wine, egg yolk)

In a heavy skillet brown lightly 3 chopped shallots and 2 tablespoons of diced lean bacon, or ham, in 2 tablespoons of butter. Add 2 veal chops and brown them slowly, turning them from time to time. When the chops are done, remove them to a heated platter, discard part of the fat in the pan and add ¼ cup of veal stock, ¼ cup white wine, and salt and pepper. Simmer the sauce briefly and thicken it at the last minute by pouring it very gradually into 1 beaten egg yolk, stirring constantly. Add a few drops of wine vinegar and 1 teaspoon of chopped parsley. Reheat the sauce carefully without letting it boil and pour it over the chops. ʼes two.

16

OLD MONTMARTRE *Paris*

Onion Soup

Soupe à l'Oignon

(Onions, stock, bread, cheese)

When you are left with the carcass of a roast chicken, boil it down with seasonings to make a stock. Then try, instead of the usual chicken soup, a Parisian *soupe à l'oignon:* In a heavy kettle sauté 4 or 5 finely sliced onions in a generous tablespoon of butter. Cook the onions until they are soft and lightly browned and stir them often as they may tend to burn. Season the onions with a little salt and pepper (remember your stock is seasoned), and pour in 5 cups of the hot stock. Simmer the soup for 5 to 8 minutes, pour it into an ovenproof casserole and float slices of French bread on top. Sprinkle the bread with plenty of grated Swiss or Parmesan cheese and brown the bread and cheese lightly under a hot broiler. Serve from the casserole. Serves four.

MARKET DAY—KAYSERSBERG   *Alsace*

Pears Amandine

Poires Amandines

(Pears, almonds, sugar syrup, strawberries, whipped cream)

Boil together 1 cup of water and ½ cup of sugar for 3 or 4 minutes and add 2 drops of vanilla. Peel 3 firm fresh pears, cut them in half and scoop out the cores. Cook the pears slowly in the syrup for 5 to 8 minutes. Arrange the pear halves in a circle on a platter, round side up, and stick several slivers of toasted almond into each one. Reduce the remaining syrup to about one-half. Add 1 cup of sliced strawberries with their juice and boil the mixture down again to a good syrupy consistency. Force the strawberry sauce through a fine sieve, spoon it carefully over the pears and chill them in the refrigerator. Serve with whipped cream.

18

HOSTELLERIE DU VIEUX PÉROUGES *Bresse*

Sautéed Veal Kidneys with Red Wine

Rognons de Veau au Vin Rouge

(Veal kidneys, onion, mushrooms, red wine, rice)

Veal kidneys must not be cooked too long or they will be tough. This recipe gives succulent results, and it will work equally well with cubes of calf's liver.

Wash 2 veal kidneys, remove all the fat, skin, and the hard center membrane, and cut the kidneys into small pieces. Brown the pieces quickly in plenty of hot butter, with salt and pepper, 1 small finely chopped onion and ¾ cup of sliced mushrooms. Sprinkle a scant tablespoon of flour over the kidneys, blend the mixture thoroughly and add ½ cup of dry red wine and ½ cup of water. Let the liquid simmer down briefly and pour the kidneys and sauce into a ring of fluffy rice. Serves four.

19

PROVINCIAL CAFÉ—VERSAILLES   *Ile-de-France*

Braised Sweetbreads

Ris de Veau Braisés au Madère

(Sweetbreads, onion, carrot, herbs, chicken stock, Madeira)

Wash 2 pairs of sweetbreads and soak them in ice water for 1 hour. Put them in a saucepan with fresh water to cover, the juice of ½ a lemon, and a little salt. Bring the water to a boil, then simmer the sweetbreads gently for 15 minutes. Drain them, chill them in ice water, and remove the tough sinews and outside membranes. Flatten the sweetbreads between two plates, weighing them down with some handy object, and keep them cold.

Use an ovenproof casserole just large enough to hold the sweetbreads without overlapping them. Melt 2 tablespoons of butter in the casserole and add 1 onion and 1 carrot, both sliced, 1 bay leaf, 2 sprigs of parsley and a pinch of thyme. When the vegetables begin to brown, blend in 1 teaspoon of flour. Season the sweetbreads with salt and pepper, arrange them on top of the vegetables, and add 1 cup of chicken stock or consommé. Bake them, uncovered, and basting occasionally, in a 400° oven for 45 minutes, or until they are brown on top and the liquid is half cooked away. Remove the sweetbreads to a hot platter. Add 2 tablespoons of Madeira to the juices in the casserole, strain this sauce over the sweetbreads and serve immediately. Serves four.

PLACE ST. LAZARE—AVALLON *Burgundy*

Chicken in Red Wine

Coq au Vin

(Chicken, onion, garlic, red wine)

In a heavy saucepan sauté 1 sliced onion and 1 minced clove of garlic in 1½ tablespoons of butter until the onion is soft. Add the neck, wing tips and giblets of a roasting chicken. When these have browned a little, add 4 cups of dry red wine and a bay leaf, cover the saucepan and simmer the mixture over the lowest possible flame for about 2 hours. Shortly before servingtime, in an iron skillet sauté the rest of the chicken, cut in serving pieces, in 2 tablespoons of butter. When the chicken is brown and almost cooked, strain the red-wine stock and blend into it 1 tablespoon of butter creamed with 2 teaspoons of flour. Pour the wine sauce over the chicken and simmer the *coq au vin*, covered, for 30 minutes. Serve with rice or boiled potatoes. Serves four to six.

HOSPICE DE BEAUNE   *Burgundy*

Liver Pâté

Pâté de Foie

(Pork, chicken livers, shallot, spices, brandy, Madeira, bacon)

An aromatic slice of *pâté maison,* served with French bread, butter and little sour pickles, is a classic hors-d'oeuvre all over France.

Put 1 pound of fresh lean pork and 1 pound of chicken livers (or ½ pound chicken livers and ½ pound calf's liver) several times through the finest blade of the meat grinder. Add 1 chopped shallot, 2 tablespoons of chopped parsley, 2 teaspoons of freshly ground pepper, ⅔ teaspoon of powdered ginger, ¼ teaspoon of cinnamon, 2¼ teaspoons of salt, 1 tablespoon of brandy and 1 tablespoon of Madeira. Mix all the ingredients together thoroughly.

Line a loaf pan with strips of bacon, pack in the pork-and-liver mixture, and bake the pâté in a 350° oven for about 1½ hours. Cool the pâté under pressure, preferably under another loaf pan containing any handy object heavy enough to pack the meat down to a firm consistency. Chill before serving.

22

THE RIVER LOIRE AT BEAUGENCY *Orléanais*

Baked Stuffed Shad

Alose au Four Gourmandine

(Shad, shallots, parsley, garlic, ham, mustard)

American fishermen will get as much pleasure from this recipe as do French anglers on the river Loire.

Chop finely together 2 shallots, a sprig of parsley and ½ clove of garlic. Add 2 tablespoons of chopped ham, gently simmer this stuffing for 3 minutes in 1 tablespoon of oil and add 1 teaspoon of prepared French mustard. Stuff a whole, dressed shad with this mixture and sew up the slit side of the fish. Slash a few shallow diagonal cuts along the top of the shad, put it in a buttered baking dish and over it pour ¼ cup of melted butter. Sprinkle the shad with salt and pepper and fine bread crumbs, and bake it in a moderately hot oven for about 25 minutes. Serve shad *gourmandine* in the baking dish, with quarters of lemon.

23

VACATION AT ST. CAST   *Brittany*

Baked Oysters with Almonds

Huîtres aux Amandes

(Oysters, almonds, butter, brandy, cayenne)

Allow about ½ cup of dressing for each dozen oysters. Cream together equal parts of finely ground blanched almonds and sweet butter. For each ½ cup of this dressing blend in thoroughly ½ a minced and crushed clove of garlic, 1½ teaspoons of brandy and a cautious sprinkling of cayenne pepper. Pour off most of the liquor from oysters on their half-shells, and cover each one with about 2 teaspoons of dressing. Bake them in a 450° oven for 5 minutes and serve immediately.

24

THATCHED FARMHOUSES—ILE-DE-FEDRUN   *Brittany*

Anchovy Baked Mashed Potatoes

Purée de Pommes de Terre aux Anchois

(Potatoes, anchovies, butter, eggs, cream, Swiss cheese, bread crumbs)

Mince 4 anchovy fillets and work them to a paste with 2 tablespoons of butter. Cut 4 more fillets into ¼-inch pieces. In a bowl mix together 2 cups of hot mashed potatoes, 2 lightly beaten egg yolks, ½ cup of warm cream, the anchovy butter and diced fillets, ¼ cup of grated Swiss cheese and a little pepper. Fold in 2 beaten egg whites and turn the mixture into a well-buttered soufflé dish. Sprinkle the top with fine bread crumbs and bake the potatoes in a preheated 375° oven for 25 minutes, or until the top is golden brown and a little puffed. Pour melted butter over the top just before serving. Serves six.

25

THE MARKET CHURCH OF ST. PIERRE—SENLIS *Ile-de-France*

Lamb Chops Argenteuil

Côtelettes d'Agneau Argenteuil

(Lamb chops, bread crumbs, asparagus tips, new potatoes)

The word Argenteuil traditionally indicates a dish served with asparagus.

Dip 6 well-trimmed lamb chops in melted butter and fine bread crumbs. In a skillet brown the chops quickly on each side in 3 tablespoons of butter; then cook them slowly until done but still juicy and a little pink in the center. Boil 4-inch asparagus tips in salted water, drain them, put them on a hot platter and pour melted butter over them. Arrange the chops in a ring around them, and around the chops place tiny new potatoes sautéed in butter. Serves six.

ROLLING FIELDS NEAR METZ *Lorraine*

Pork Tenderloin Lorraine

Filet de Porc Lorraine

(Pork tenderloin, bread crumbs, onion, shallot, garlic, parsley, stock, vinegar)

In a small roasting pan on top of the stove brown a lean pork tenderloin on all sides in 2 tablespoons of butter. Cover the tenderloin with a generous layer of fine bread crumbs mixed with salt and pepper. Mince 1 onion, 1 shallot, 1 clove of garlic, and 2 or 3 sprigs of parsley, and sprinkle them on the meat. Put the roast in a hot oven to brown the layer of bread crumbs, basting it several times with melted butter. Once the crumbs are brown, lower the oven temperature to medium, add 1 cup of stock to the pan, cover it, and bake the meat until it is done, or for about 50 minutes. Then uncover the pan, raise the oven temperature and brown the crumbs again for another 10 minutes. Put the roast on a hot platter, and stir 1 tablespoon of wine vinegar into the sauce before serving it. Serves four.

PALAIS DU GOUVERNEMENT—NANCY *Lorraine*

Brussels Sprouts and Chestnuts

Choux de Bruxelles Sautés aux Marrons

(Brussels sprouts, chestnuts, butter, consommé)

Prepare ½ pound of boiled chestnuts, or use well-drained canned chestnuts. Trim 1 pound of firm Brussels sprouts and soak them in salted water. Boil them in fresh salted water for 15 minutes, or until they are just tender, and drain them. In a skillet sauté the chestnuts in 2 tablespoons of hot butter until they are nicely browned. Add the Brussels sprouts and more butter if necessary. When the sprouts take on a little color, moisten with ¼ cup strong beef consommé and simmer all together until the liquid is reduced. Serves four to six.

28

THE RIVER DOUBS   *Franche-Comté*

Cheese and Ham Stuffed Rolls

Petits Pains au Fromage

(Soft rolls, milk, cheese, ham, butter)

Serve these *petits pains* at a buffet supper or with cocktails.

Use the smallest available soft rolls, or cut larger ones in halves or quarters just before serving them. Split the rolls in half horizontally and scrape out as much of the soft centers as you can without damaging the crusts. Prepare a mixture of equal parts of freshly grated cheese and minced ham. Moisten the soft bread crumbs with a very little boiling milk and mix them with an equal amount of the cheese and ham mixture. Stuff and reassemble the split rolls and arrange them on a buttered cooky sheet. Brush the tops with melted butter, and heat the rolls in a slow oven until the cheese has melted and they just begin to toast. Serve the pieces of halved or quartered rolls on toothpicks.

29

GATEWAY TO DIANE DE POITIERS' CHÂTEAU—ANET *Orléanais*

Hot Cheese and Ham Sandwiches

Croque Monsieur

(Bread, Swiss cheese, ham, cream, butter, cream sauce)

Trim the crusts from thin slices of white bread. Mix grated Swiss cheese with just enough heavy cream to make a paste and spread a generous layer of it on each piece of bread. Put the slices together into sandwiches, with a thin slice of ham in between. Dip the sandwiches in beaten egg and sauté them in hot butter until they are crisp and golden on each side. Make a cream sauce with 1 tablespoon of butter, melted and blended with 1 teaspoon of flour, 1 cup of cream, stirred in gradually, 2 tablespoons of grated Swiss cheese, and salt and pepper. Blend the cream sauce well, let it thicken slightly and serve it over the *croque monsieur*.

VILLAGE SCHOOLHOUSE, ONCE A SMALL CHÂTEAU   *Champagne*
—RUMILLY

Cream of Cucumber Soup

Potage Crème de Concombre

(Cucumbers, milk, potato starch, egg yolks, cream, chives or dill)

Peel 2 fresh cucumbers, cut them lengthwise, scoop out the seeds and cut the cucumbers into 1-inch pieces. Sprinkle the pieces with salt, let them stand for several hours, drain them, drop them into 2 cups of boiling water, and let them cook for 5 minutes. Drain the cucumbers again, reserve the cooking water, and sauté them gently for 5 minutes in 1 tablespoon of butter. Do not let the butter brown. Force the cucumbers through a fine sieve and add 1½ cups of the cooking water and 1½ cups of milk. Add 1 tablespoon of potato starch dissolved in a little milk, and salt and pepper to taste. Beat 2 egg yolks with 3 tablespoons of heavy cream and pour a little of the cucumber soup into this mixture to blend it without cooking the eggs. Pour the eggs and cream into the soup and heat it, stirring, until it is slightly thickened. Do not let it boil. Serve the *crème de concombre* with a sprinkling of chopped chives or dill. Serves four.

TOUR GABRIEL—RAMPARTS OF MONT ST. MICHEL   *Normandy*

Lobster in Cream

Homard à la Crème

(Lobster, brandy, seasoning, egg yolks, cream, sherry)

Slice the meat of a 2-pound boiled lobster and heat the pieces in 2 tablespoons of hot butter for 1 or 2 minutes. Add salt, pepper and a little paprika. Pour on 1 tablespoon of warmed brandy, set it aflame and shake the pan back and forth until the flame dies. Beat 2 egg yolks with ¾ cup of cream, add 2 tablespoons of sherry and pour this sauce over the lobster. Keep the lobster over a low fire, stirring constantly, until the sauce thickens, but do not let it boil. Serves two.

VILLAGE FOUNTAIN—RIQUEWIHR   *Alsace*

Beef à la Mode

Boeuf à la Mode

(Beef, white wine, herbs, veal knuckle, brandy, carrots, onions)

Boeuf à la mode is one of the most delicious commonplaces of French cooking. Serve it hot one day and cold the next, when the sauce will have jelled rather like an aspic.

Remove the fat from a 4-pound piece of beef suitable for a pot roast. Run a few narrow strips of salt pork through it with a larding needle. In a deep iron casserole brown the meat on all sides in 1 tablespoon of butter. Add 1 cup of hot water, 2 cups of white wine, salt and pepper, a bay leaf, a sprig of parsley, a good pinch of thyme, a pinch of nutmeg, and a piece of cracked veal knuckle. Simmer the beef, covered, over a low flame for about 2 hours, then add 2 tablespoons of brandy, 4 carrots, cut in pieces, and 6 small whole onions. Stick 2 or 3 cloves into one of the onions. Simmer the *boeuf à la mode* for another 1½ hours, or until it is tender. Remove the veal knuckle and the cloves before serving. The sauce should be fairly brown and rich; if there is too much, pour it into another pan and reduce it over a brisk flame.

33

BASQUE COUNTRY TOWN—USTARITZ *Pyrenees*

Basque Omelette

Pipérade

(Eggs, green pepper, onion, tomato, ham)

A *pipérade* is neither quite an omelette nor quite scrambled eggs, but something in between. And it is neither quite French nor quite Spanish — it is Basque.

In 2 tablespoons of oil sauté 1 small green pepper and 1 small onion, both thinly sliced, 1 small clove of garlic, chopped and mashed, and 1 large ripe tomato, peeled, seeded and chopped. Add 2 tablespoons of chopped ham and let the mixture simmer over a low fire for 20 to 30 minutes. When the vegetables are soft, stir in 1 tablespoon of butter, let it melt and pour in 4 lightly beaten eggs. Add more salt and pepper if necessary, stir just once or twice, let the eggs set and serve the *pipérade* from the pan. Serves two.

BARLES, A MOUNTAIN VILLAGE   *Dauphiny*

Scalloped Potatoes

Gratin Dauphinois

(Potatoes, milk or cream, seasoning)

The secret of this dish is to slice the potatoes paper-thin and to cook them just long enough to brown them on top without drying them out underneath. The recipe is very simple, and yet it may require practice.

Slice raw potatoes very thinly and spread the slices in layers in a shallow baking dish. Sprinkle a little salt and pepper on each layer and add a dash of nutmeg if you like it. Fill the dish with milk, or even better, with thin cream, just to the level of the top layer of potatoes. Dot the *gratin* with bits of butter and bake it in a very slow oven for 1¼ to 1½ hours, or just to the point where the milk is all absorbed, the potatoes are soft and the top layer is delicately browned. Serve from the baking dish.

35

PONT ST. BÉNÉZET—AVIGNON   *Provence*

Braised Beef Avignon

Boeuf à la Façon d'Avignon

(Beef, herbs, white wine, bacon, shallots, onions, tomato, mushrooms)

Marinate a 4-pound piece of beef (top of the round, rump, or a similar piece) with ½ lemon, sliced, 2 cloves of garlic, cut in pieces, a good pinch of thyme, 1 bay leaf, ½ teaspoon each of chopped tarragon and chives, a little pepper, 2 cups of white wine and 4 tablespoons of olive oil. Let the meat stand for 12 hours and turn it from time to time in the marinade.

Put the beef in an earthen casserole with a piece of bacon rind under it. Add 4 shallots, cut in pieces, 3 or 4 peeled and seeded tomatoes, cut in quarters, 2 cloves of garlic, chopped, 6 or 8 small onions, 2 tablespoons of diced bacon, ¼ pound of mushrooms, and a sprig of parsley. Pour 1 cup of beef stock and the marinade over the beef. This dish should be cooked in the slowest possible oven for 5 to 6 hours. For best results the casserole should be hermetically sealed. The French way of doing this is to make a paste of flour and water, shape it into a long, narrow roll, fit the roll around the edge of the casserole and press the lid firmly down upon it.

AMBOISE   *Touraine*

Salmon in White Wine

Saumon au Vin Blanc

(Salmon steaks, white wine, butter, steamed potatoes, green peas)

In the Touraine this dish is made with Vouvray, but any good dry, white table wine will do. For a Gallic version of the American 4th of July salmon-and-green peas, why not serve *saumon au vin blanc* with *petits pois à la française?*

In a heavy skillet brown 4 salmon steaks on each side in plenty of butter. Add salt and a little pepper and when the salmon is half cooked, pour in 1½ cups of white wine. Simmer the steaks over a brisk fire until the butter and wine are reduced to a rich but still juicy sauce. Serve the salmon with steamed potatoes and green peas.

Here is the incomparable French method for preparing peas: In a covered pan, over a low flame, simmer 2 cups of green peas in ¼ cup of water with 4 green lettuce leaves, 1 small sliced onion, 2 tablespoons of butter, a sprig of parsley, ¼ teaspoon of sugar, a pinch of thyme, and salt and pepper to taste. The peas should be tender and the liquid almost absorbed in about ½ hour. Serves four.

ALPHONSE DAUDET'S WINDMILL—FONTVIEILLE   *Provence*

Eggplant and Tomato Hors-d'Oeuvre

Aubergine à la Turque

(Eggplant, tomatoes, onions, peppercorns, olive oil)

A la turque here means a general Mediterranean style. Eggplant is often served this way in the south of France.

Peel an eggplant and slice it rather thinly. Salt the slices, pile them together, let them stand under pressure for ½ hour, and drain off the liquid. Peel and slice 6 large ripe tomatoes and 3 or 4 onions. In the bottom of a shallow baking dish arrange a layer of onion slices, put a layer of eggplant over the onions, then a layer of tomato over the eggplant. Sprinkle in a few whole peppercorns and a little salt. Keep this up until you have used all of the vegetables, finishing off with a layer of tomato slices each neatly decorated with a round of onion. Fill all the corners and empty spaces with bits of tomato. Fill the dish just to the top layer of tomato with olive oil, and bake it in a 250° oven for 3 hours or more. Baste the juices over the top several times. Serve chilled.

VILLAGE DRY-DOCK—YPORT *Normandy*

Scallops Saint-Jacques

Coquilles Saint-Jacques

(Scallops, shallot, white wine, parsley, bread crumbs, cheese)

Slice ¾ pint of sea scallops. Sauté the pieces gently for 3 minutes in 2 table-spoons of butter with a little pepper and 1 chopped shallot. Add 2 tablespoons of fine bread crumbs and ¾ cup of white wine, and simmer the scallops for 8 to 10 minutes, or until the sauce is slightly reduced and thickened. Add 1 teaspoon of finely chopped parsley, and salt if necessary, and fill 4 scallop shells with the mixture. Sprinkle the *coquilles* with bread crumbs and grated Parmesan, dot them with butter and brown them lightly under a hot broiler. Serves four.

THE NORTH PORCH OF THE CATHEDRAL
OF NOTRE-DAME—CHARTRES

Blanquette of Veal

Blanquette de Veau

(Veal, onion, carrots, mushrooms, egg yolks)

A *blanquette de veau* is a veal stew almost too delicate to be called a stew. Every cook in France knows the recipe well.

Cut 1½ pounds of young, white stewing veal into cubes and put the meat in a bowl with boiling water to cover. Put a lid on the bowl and let the meat stand for 20 minutes. Drain off the water and put the veal in a heavy saucepan with 2 onions and 2 carrots, all cut in pieces, salt and pepper and a sprig of parsley, and cover the veal again with boiling water. Simmer the *blanquette*, covered, over a low fire for about 1½ hours. Then add ½ pound of sliced mushrooms and simmer for another ½ hour. In a separate saucepan melt 1 tablespoon of butter, blend in 1 tablespoon of flour and stir in gradually 2 cups of the veal stock. Simmer this sauce until it is slightly reduced. Beat 2 egg yolks in a bowl with 1 teaspoon of lemon juice and add the hot sauce gradually. Return the mixture to the saucepan and stir it over a very low flame until it just begins to thicken. The sauce should be almost white. Pour it over the meat and vegetables, which have been drained and kept hot, and serve the *blanquette* with rice. Serves four.

TAKING ON SUPPLIES—CAMARET-SUR-MER *Brittany*

Cod Brittany

Cabillaud à la Bretonne

(Codfish, cider, parsley, shallots, mushrooms)

Put a 2-pound piece of fresh cod, boned and skinned, in a baking dish first greased with 3 tablespoons of salad oil. Sprinkle the fish with salt and pepper and with 2 shallots, 1 teaspoon of parsley, and 4 or 5 mushrooms, all chopped. Add 2 cups of hard cider. Work 1 teaspoon of flour to a smooth paste with 1 tablespoon of butter and add it to the cider. Bake the codfish in a moderately hot oven and baste it several times. It should be done in 20 to 30 minutes. Serves four.

SCREEN OF POPLARS—OZENAY

Burgundy

Duck with Olives

Canard aux Olives

(Duck, Italian vermouth, olives)

Spread a duck with softened butter, salt and pepper it, and roast it in a hot oven. Add ½ cup of water and ½ cup of sweet Italian vermouth to the fat in the pan and baste the duck often. Fifteen minutes before the duck is done, add 1 cup of small pitted green Italian olives. Serve the duck and the olives together. Skim most of the fat from the pan juices and serve them in a sauceboat.

PASTORALE   *Normandy*

Creamed Camembert Cheese

Crème de Camembert

(Camembert, white wine, butter)

Crème de camembert will be at its best if it is served with French bread and
a bottle of red wine.

Take a ripe Camembert cheese (whole or in sections), scrape off the skin
carefully and thoroughly and let the cheese stand in a bowl, covered with dry
white wine, for 12 hours. Drain it, wipe it dry and cream it thoroughly with ⅓
cup of sweet butter. Shape the Camembert cream into the form of the original
cheese, coat it on all sides with very fine toast crumbs and chill it well before
serving.

RAMPARTS OF THE CHÂTEAU—FARCHEVILLE *Ile-de-France*

Baked Eggs with Mushrooms

Oeufs Bonne Femme

(Croutons, mushrooms, butter, eggs)

Cut slices of good white bread into circles about 3 inches across. Sauté the circles in butter until they are crisp and brown on both sides. In another skillet, over a low flame, sauté finely minced mushrooms in butter until they are soft and the liquid they give off is reduced. Arrange the sautéed croutons close together in a shallow, buttered baking dish, spread them with the cooked mushrooms and carefully break an egg over each one. Season with salt and pepper and bake the *oeufs bonne femme* in a 350° oven for 10 minutes, or until the whites are set but the yolks are still soft.

44

THE OLD AUBERGE—BEAULIEU-SUR-DORDOGNE *Limousin*

Puréed Vegetable Soup

Potage aux Légumes

(Onion, carrots, turnips, potatoes, celery, butter, cream)

In a large saucepan sauté 1 large sliced onion in 1 tablespoon of butter until it is soft and lightly browned. Add 2 carrots, 2 small white turnips, 3 medium potatoes and 2 stalks of celery, all cut in small pieces, a sprig of parsley, and salt and pepper. Cook the vegetables for a few minutes in the butter, stirring often. Then add 5 cups of hot water, cover the saucepan and simmer the soup over a low flame for 1 hour. Pass the soup through a sieve into another saucepan, and force through all the vegetables. To serve this traditional French *potage*, reheat it with a big lump of butter and add 2 tablespoons of extra-heavy sweet or sour cream. Serves six.

THE CHÄTEAU AND THE HORSESHOE STAIRCASE   *Ile-de-France*
—FONTAINEBLEAU

Artichokes with Mousseline Sauce

Artichauts, Sauce Mousseline

(Artichokes, and a sauce of eggs, butter, lemon juice, cream)

Cover 6 handsome artichokes with boiling salted water and cook them for about 45 minutes, or until the bases are tender when pricked with a sharp knife. Drain them and serve them hot. Eat the ends of the artichoke leaves and the bases with a frothy *sauce mousseline:*

In an earthenware bowl lightly beat 4 egg yolks with 4 tablespoons of cream. Fit the bowl into the top of a pan of barely simmering water. Let the yolks thicken slightly, stirring them constantly with a wire whisk. Divide ¼ pound of butter into 4 pieces and stir in the pieces one at a time, letting each one melt before adding the next. When the eggs and butter have thickened somewhat, take the bowl off the pan of hot water, stir in 2 teaspoons of lemon juice and a pinch each of salt and pepper. Add about ¾ cup of stiffly whipped cream. Put the bowl back over the hot water and stir the sauce, very gently this time, until it is hot. If the flame under the pan of water is low enough and the earthenware bowl is thick enough, there should be no danger of this *sauce mousseline* curdling. Serves six.

HARVEST—NEAR LUSSAC-LE-CHÂTEAU

Fowl with Rice

Poule au Riz

(Fowl, herbs, vegetables, rice, egg yolks)

Put a whole, dressed fowl in a deep kettle with salt, pepper, parsley, 1 bay leaf, a pinch of thyme, 2 cloves of garlic, 1 stalk of celery and 1 quartered onion. Add water to cover, put the lid on the kettle and simmer the fowl gently for about 2 hours, or until it is tender.

Wash 1½ cups of rice and cook it in 3 cups of stock from the chicken pot. Add a little more stock if the liquid is absorbed before the rice is tender. Beat 2 egg yolks in the top of a double boiler, add gradually 2 cups of the chicken stock, strained, and heat the sauce over simmering water. Stir the sauce with a whisk until it just begins to thicken and ad 1 tablespoon of butter. Put the rice on a hot platter, carve the chicken and put the pieces on the bed of rice. Serve the sauce separately. Serves six.

ROMAN ARCH (49 B.C.)—ORANGE *Provence*

Grilled Pepper Hors-d'Oeuvre

Poivrons Grillés

(Green peppers, olive oil, French dressing, onion)

Split large green peppers in half lengthwise and remove the stems, seeds and all the white membranes. Soak the peppers in a little olive oil for 30 minutes; then drain them and broil them under a low flame, turning them occasionally, until they are slightly browned and blistered. (Ideally this should be done over a charcoal fire.) Cut the peppers into thin strips and sprinkle them with a little finely minced onion. Marinate them for an hour or more in a French dressing made of 1 part vinegar, 3 parts olive oil, and mustard, salt and pepper to taste, and serve them cold but not chilled.

REFLECTED LANDSCAPE NEAR LANNE   *Pyrenees*

Cucumber Hors-d'Oeuvre

Concombres à la Grecque

(Cucumbers, salad oil, lemon juice, herbs, spices)

Peel 2 large or 3 small cucumbers, quarter them lengthwise, scoop out the
seeds and cut the quarters into 1-inch pieces. Heat to the boiling point 1 cup
of water, 6 tablespoons of salad oil and the juice of 2 lemons with a *bouquet
garni* composed of parsley, celery leaves, thyme, a bay leaf, and a stalk of fennel
or some fennel seeds, adding also salt, pepper and a dozen coriander seeds. Add
the cucumbers and cook them over a medium flame for 10 minutes. Remove the
bouquet garni and cool the cucumbers in the cooking liquid. Serve them chilled,
with just enough liquid to serve as a dressing. Serves four.

THE CHÂTEAU AT CHANTILLY *Ile-de-France*

Strawberries with Whipped Cream

Fraises Chantilly

(Strawberries, cream, powdered sugar, vanilla)

Hull a basket of ripe strawberries and cut them in half. Stir them into a bowl of fluffy whipped cream flavored with a little powdered sugar and vanilla. The cream should not be too stiff and there should be enough of it to smother the strawberries completely. Let the *fraises Chantilly* stand in the refrigerator for 2 hours before serving them. They will be nicely chilled and the cream will be streaked with pink strawberry juice.

THE ROOFTOPS OF CHINON *Touraine*

Caramel Custard

Crème Renversée

(Eggs, sugar, milk, vanilla)

Heat ½ cup of sugar in a heavy pan over moderate heat until it melts and browns, stirring it constantly. Add very slowly ½ cup of boiling water, stirring to keep it from boiling over. Simmer the caramel for 2 or 3 minutes and pour it into a china or glass baking dish, turning and tilting the dish to coat all the inside. Beat 2 whole eggs and 3 egg yolks in a bowl with a pinch of salt, 4 tablespoons granulated sugar and 1 teaspoon of vanilla. Stir in gradually 1½ cups of hot milk. Pour this custard into the baking dish. Set the dish in a shallow pan of water and bake the custard for 1 hour in a 250° oven. It will be done when a knife inserted in the center comes out clean. Serve the *crème renversée* chilled and turned out on a platter. The caramel will cover it like a sauce.

PALACE OF THE POPES—AVIGNON   *Provence*

Avignon Flambéed Filets Mignons

Filets Mignons Flambés à l'Avignonnaise

(Beef tenderloin, garlic, butter, croutons, brandy)

Rub slices of beef tenderloin, cut 1½ inches thick, on both sides with a cut clove of garlic. Season them generously with salt and coarsely ground pepper. Sauté circles of bread, cut to fit the filets, in plenty of butter until the croutons are crisp and brown on both sides. In a separate skillet, cook the filets in hot butter over a high flame. They should be very brown, but also very rare inside. Then slip a crouton under each filet and add a little melted butter to the pan. Pour in about 1 teaspoon of warmed brandy for each filet, put a match to it, and shake the pan until the flame dies out. Transfer croutons and filets to a large hot platter, pour on the pan juices, and garnish the platter with water cress, broiled tomatoes, and French-fried shoe-string potatoes.

HARNESS SHOP—NOGENT-LE-ROI *Orléanais*

Cauliflower Purée

Purée de Chou-fleur

(Cauliflower, mashed potatoes, cream, butter, parsley)

Trim off the leaves and the tough end of the stem of a firm, white cauliflower. Soak it head down in salted water for ½ hour, and boil it in fresh salted water for about 20 minutes, or until the core is just tender. Drain it, mash it through a colander, and reheat it to reduce any excess liquid. Combine the purée with approximately the same amount of mashed potatoes, and add a little heavy cream and plenty of butter. Beat well with a wooden spoon and serve very hot with another lump of butter and sprinkled with parsley. Serves six.

THE SEINE AND THE PONT MARIE   *Paris*

Leek and Potato Soup

Potage Parisien

(Leeks, potatoes, cream, herbs)

Clean 2 large leeks, remove most of the green tops and slice the rest very thinly. Peel 3 potatoes and cut them into small dice. Melt 1 tablespoon butter in a saucepan, add the leeks and cook them over a low flame for 5 minutes without letting them brown. Add the potatoes and cook another minute. Then add 1½ quarts of boiling water and a little salt and simmer the soup gently for 30 minutes, skimming off the surface once or twice. The soup should reduce to about 1 quart. Stir in 1 teaspoon of butter and 3 tablespoons of heavy cream and taste for seasoning. Serve with a sprinkling of chopped chives or parsley. Serves four.

THE YACHT BASIN AT CANNES *Riviera*

Niçoise Salad

Salade Niçoise

(Lettuce, vegetables, eggs, anchovies, black olives, tuna fish)

A *salade niçoise* should be pretty as a picture when it comes to the table, but you must then courageously spoil the picture by tossing the salad thoroughly before serving it. Rub a wooden salad bowl with a cut clove of garlic. On a bed of lettuce in the bowl arrange the following traditional ingredients: 4 quartered small red tomatoes, 1 cup of cooked green beans, 2 sliced boiled potatoes, 2 quartered hard-boiled eggs, thin slices of mild Spanish onion and of green pepper, 8 anchovy fillets cut in small pieces, 10 black Italian olives, and pieces of white canned tuna fish. Over all of this pour the standard French dressing made of salt and freshly ground black pepper to taste, ½ teaspoon of prepared mustard, 2 tablespoons of red wine vinegar, and 6 tablespoons of olive oil. Serves four.

THE PORT OF AURAY *Brittany*

Lobster Alexander

Homard Alexandre

(Cold lobster, and a sauce of herbs, seasoning, eggs, oil, vinegar)

Slice the meat of a boiled lobster and arrange it on a platter. Mix ½ teaspoon each of chopped chervil, parsley, tarragon and chives with the mashed yolks of 2 hard-boiled eggs. Add salt and pepper, a little English mustard, 1 tablespoon of wine vinegar and a few drops of Worcestershire sauce. When the mixture is smoothly blended, add gradually about ½ cup of cold olive oil, stirring constantly until the sauce thickens into a sort of mayonnaise. Add a few drops of Madeira or sherry and drop a neat spoonful of sauce on each piece of lobster just before serving.

THE CHÂTEAU AT DUINGT—LAC D'ANNECY *Savoy*

Trout with Almonds and Cream

Truite aux Amandes

(Trout, almonds, cream)

Clean, wash and dry 4 small fresh trout (or 2 large ones), dip them lightly in flour and sauté them on both sides in plenty of hot butter. Remove the trout to a hot platter when they are brown. In the butter left in the pan (add more if the pan is dry) lightly brown ½ cup of blanched and slivered almonds. Add ½ cup of heavy cream, stir it briskly so it will take up the brown color of the butter, let the liquid reduce a little, and pour this sauce over the trout. Serves four.

NOTRE-DAME DE PARIS   *Paris*

Mushroom Salad

Salade de Champignons

(Mushrooms, French dressing, herbs)

This is an exceptionally delicious salad. In France it is usually found on the tray of assorted hors-d'oeuvre served as a first course.

Wash and dry, but do not peel, firm white mushroom caps. Slice them thinly, pour French dressing over them, toss them carefully and let them stand a while to absorb the dressing. Sprinkle them with chopped chives and parsley before serving. The usual French dressing of salt, pepper, 1 part red wine vinegar and 3 parts olive oil may be varied for *salade de champignons* by using a little less vinegar and adding a little lemon juice.

GOTHIC CHURCH AT ST. RIQUIER   *Picardy*

Roast Goose with Fruit Stuffing

Oie Rôtie aux Pruneaux

(Goose, onion, orange, apple, prunes, bread crumbs, seasoning)

Sauté 2 chopped onions in 3 tablespoons of butter until they are soft, add salt and pepper and 1 peeled, coarsely chopped orange. Simmer this mixture for 3 minutes and add 3 large apples and 14 large soaked and pitted prunes, all coarsely chopped. Add 2 tablespoons of sugar, ½ teaspoon each of thyme and marjoram, ¼ teaspoon each of cinnamon and nutmeg, and 1 tablespoon each of brandy and Madeira. Mix in thoroughly the chopped liver of the goose, 2 cups of coarse dry bread crumbs soaked with ¼ cup of milk, and add a little more salt and pepper. Rub the inside of the goose with salt and a little sage and thyme and pack it loosely with the stuffing. Roast the goose in a 325° oven, allowing 20 to 25 minutes per pound. Prick the skin well all over to allow the fat to run out. When the goose is ready, put it on a hot platter, skim most of the fat from the pan juices and stir in a cup of stock made from the giblets and neck, simmered in water with 1 onion, salt and pepper and a bay leaf. Reduce the sauce and serve it separately.

59

THE FARM GATE—MANOIR DE QUERVILLE   *Normandy*

Fried Cheese Puffs

Délicieuses au Fromage

(Swiss cheese, egg whites, bread crumbs)

This is a delectable hot hors-d'oeuvre. Make a paste of 2 lightly beaten egg whites mixed with ¼ pound of grated Swiss cheese. Form the paste into little balls no bigger than marbles, roll them in fine bread crumbs and fry them in very hot, deep oil. The *délicieuses* will puff up and become light and delicious, just as their name implies. Serve them immediately, with French-fried parsley.

THE NOBLE DOVECOTE, MANOIR D'ANGO—NEAR DIEPPE   *Normandy*

Omelette with Herbs

Omelette Fines Herbes

(Eggs, parsley, chives, tarragon, chervil)

Add 1 tablespoon of water and a little salt and pepper to 6 eggs and beat them briefly with a fork. Stir in 1 teaspoon each of finely chopped parsley, chives, tarragon and chervil. Put 1 tablespoon of butter in an omelette pan just hot enough to make the butter sizzle but not brown. Pour in the eggs and stir them twice quickly with the flat of the fork. Shake the pan to keep the omelette free. As soon as it is set but still soft, fold over one edge of the omelette with a spatula. Slide the unfolded edge right out of the pan onto a platter, then turn the pan completely over the platter. The omelette should land with two edges neatly tucked under and the top golden and unbroken. It should be cooked through but quite soft.

REFLECTIONS IN THE RIVER TARN—ALBI *Languedoc*

Beef Tongue with Sauce Piquante

Langue de Boeuf, Sauce Piquante

(Beef tongue, shallots, wine vinegar, white wine, herbs, capers, pickles)

Wash and scrape a fresh beef tongue and cook it slowly in a large kettle with 3 or more quarts of water, salt, several peppercorns, 1 onion, cut in half, 1 carrot, cut in pieces, parsley, 1 bay leaf, and a good pinch of thyme. Simmer the tongue for about 3 hours. Then skin it and serve it sliced and garnished with water cress.

With *langue de boeuf* serve this spicy *sauce piquante:* Simmer 4 finely chopped shallots in ¼ cup of wine vinegar and ¼ cup of white wine. Add salt and pepper to taste. When the liquid is reduced to about one-half, add 1 cup of the stock in which the tongue was cooked and simmer the sauce 10 minutes longer. In a small bowl dissolve 1 teaspoon of potato flour in a little of the tongue stock and stir this mixture into the sauce to thicken it slightly. Add 2 teaspoons of fresh herbs (parsley, tarragon and chervil) and 1 small sour pickle, all finely chopped, 1 teaspoon of capers and a little freshly ground pepper.

SIXTEENTH-CENTURY STREET CORNER—BOURGES   *Berry*

Germaine's Creamed Spinach with Madeira
Epinards au Madère à la Germaine
(Spinach, mushrooms, cream, Madeira, croutons)

Epinards au madère is no ordinary vegetable; it deserves to be eaten as a separate course.

Cook 2 pounds of spinach, covered, with ¼ cup of water for about 10 minutes, or until it is just soft. Drain it thoroughly and put it through the finest blade of the meat grinder. Drain the spinach again, add 1 tablespoon of butter, a dash of nutmeg, salt and pepper, and ¼ cup of heavy cream. Sauté ¼ pound of sliced mushrooms in 1 tablespoon of butter for 4 or 5 minutes, add them to the spinach and stir in 2 tablespoons of Madeira. Sauté 1 cup of diced white bread in 2 tablespoons of butter until the croutons are crisp and golden brown. Reheat the spinach and sprinkle it with the croutons. Serves four.

63

THE INNER PORT—HONFLEUR *Normandy*

Fillets of Flounder in White Wine

Filets de Sole au Vin Blanc

(Flounder fillets, white wine, shallot, mushrooms, cream, egg yolks)

Spread 1½ pounds of fillets of flounder in a shallow baking dish. Add 1 cup of dry white wine, sprinkle the fillets with salt and pepper and add 1 finely chopped shallot and ¼ pound of sliced mushrooms. Dot the fish with butter and bake it in a moderate oven for 20 minutes, or until it is cooked but still firm. Drain off the liquid in the baking dish and simmer it down to about 1 cup. Mix 2 egg yolks with ½ cup of heavy cream and stir them carefully into the reduced fish stock. Add 1 teaspoon of chopped parsley, pour the sauce over the flounder and glaze it briefly under a hot broiler. Serves four.

THE FORTIFIED BRIDGE—CAHORS   *Gascony*

Chestnut Pudding

Mont-Blanc

(Chestnuts, milk, sugar, vanilla, egg yolks, butter, whipped cream)

Slash the shells of 2 pounds of chestnuts on the flat side. Put the chestnuts in a frying pan with a little hot oil and heat them until the shells begin to loosen. Let them cool, peel them and boil them in salted water for 10 minutes; drain them and remove the remaining bits of the inner skin. Cover the chestnuts with 2¼ cups of milk, add ½ teaspoon of vanilla and 6 tablespoons of sugar, and boil them gently until they are soft. Force the mixture through a colander and add 2 tablespoons of butter and enough hot milk to give the purée a moderately thick consistency. Mix it thoroughly and let it cool. Then add 2 egg yolks and chill it in the refrigerator. Shape the chestnut purée into a low pyramid on a serving platter and cover it with sweetened whipped cream.

THE PALACE OF VERSAILLES   *Ile-de-France*

Francine's Chocolate Cream

Marquise au Chocolat à la Francine

(Milk, sugar, eggs, butter, chocolate)

Over a low flame dissolve ½ cup of granulated sugar in a scant ½ cup of milk. Put in a vanilla bean for a little while for flavor, or use a few drops of vanilla extract. When the milk has boiled, let it cool and stir it into 3 beaten egg yolks. Thicken the custard over barely simmering water and stir it constantly. Put it aside to cool.

Put ¾ of a pound of unsalted butter in a bowl and cream it until it is very soft. (This may take about ½ hour.) Melt ¼ pound of bittersweet chocolate with 2 tablespoons of water in the top of a double boiler. Let the chocolate cool and stir it a little at a time into the creamed butter. Add the cooled custard, and then settle down to some 20 minutes of constant stirring. This may seem like a lot of work, but the *marquise* will acquire a beautiful consistency. Pour the *marquise* into a mold and chill it. Unmold it onto a platter and serve a small slice to each guest (this is a very, very rich dessert) with the following custard sauce: Boil 2 cups of milk with 6 lumps of sugar and a vanilla bean. When the sugar is dissolved, remove the vanilla bean, cool the milk a little and stir it slowly into 6 beaten egg yolks. Thicken the sauce over simmering water, stirring constantly, and serve it cold.

INFORMAL FARM ARCHITECTURE *Guyenne*

Steak with Bordelaise Sauce

Steak Bordelaise

(Steak, shallot, red wine, stock, herbs, lemon)

The French seldom bother about outdoor barbecue cooking, but it just so happens that this great French provincial recipe is perfection for a charcoal-broiled steak. The sauce can be made ahead of time in the kitchen.

Broil a good thick steak over a charcoal fire until it is brown on both sides but rare in the center. Carve it and serve it with this *sauce bordelaise:* Combine 1 chopped shallot, freshly ground pepper, ¼ teaspoon salt, a pinch each of marjoram and thyme, and a small bay leaf with ½ cup of red wine. Simmer this mixture until the wine is reduced to about half its original quantity. Now add ½ cup of good strong beef stock and reduce the sauce again to about one-half. Add ½ teaspoon lemon juice, strain the sauce through a fine sieve, add a good lump of butter and 1 teaspoon of chopped parsley. A true *sauce bordelaise* also contains sliced marrow from the center of a boiled marrowbone, but this is not absolutely necessary.

ARC DE TRIOMPHE   *Paris*

Chicken Salad Boulestin

Salade de Poulet Boulestin

(Rice, cold chicken, French dressing, peppers, mayonnaise, mustard, eggs, herbs)

For leftover chicken deluxe: Season freshly boiled rice while it is still hot with a French dressing made of 1 part wine vinegar, 3 parts olive oil, salt, pepper and a little prepared mustard. Mix in a little green pepper and sweet pimento, both minced, and cool the rice thoroughly. Just before serving, put the rice in a glass bowl, cover it with diced cooked chicken, and cover the chicken with homemade mayonnaise spiced with a little mustard. Decorate the salad with a circle of hardboiled egg slices and sprinkle it with chopped fresh tarragon, chives and parsley. Mix the *salade de poulet* thoroughly at the table. There should be plenty of French dressing and not too much mayonnaise.

68

CATHEDRAL OF ST. MAURICE—ANGERS

Anjou

Artichoke Hearts and Peas

Artichauts à la Clamart

(Frozen artichoke hearts, green peas, butter, herbs)

Thaw a package of frozen artichoke hearts, cut them in half lengthwise, and pat them dry in a cloth. Sauté them slowly in 2 tablespoons of butter until they are lightly browned, turning them several times. Add 2 cups of green peas, ½ cup of water, 1 tablespoon of butter, a *bouquet garni,* a pinch of sugar, and salt and pepper. Cover and simmer together over a very low flame for 25 minutes, or until the peas are tender and the liquid has almost evaporated. Serves four.

THE MARKET—PARTHENAY   *Poitou*

Cream of Cauliflower Soup
Potage Crème de Choufleur

(Cauliflower, milk, egg yolks)

Wash a cauliflower and break it into pieces. Cook the pieces in boiling salted water until they are soft but still whole, drain off the water and reserve it. Force the cauliflower through a fine sieve and add to it enough liquid (half cauliflower water and half chicken stock) to make a moderately thick soup. Simmer the soup for about 15 minutes, take it off the fire and add gradually 1 cup of milk beaten with 2 egg yolks. Add a lump of butter and reheat the soup very slowly, stirring constantly. Do not let it boil or the egg will turn. Serves four.

MEDIEVAL BUTCHER SHOP—BESSE-EN-CHANDESSE *Auvergne*

Pork Chops with Piquante Sauce

Côtelettes de Porc, Sauce Piquante

(Pork chops, onions, vinegar, pickles, Madeira)

In a heavy skillet brown 4 trimmed pork chops in butter on each side. Add 3 coarsely chopped onions and salt and pepper, and cook the onions and chops together until the onions are browned. Remove the chops. Add 1 tablespoon of flour to the pan, blend it into the juices and let this *roux* brown a little more. Stir in gradually 1 cup of water and add 1 teaspoon of vinegar and 2 or 3 small sliced sour pickles. Simmer the sauce for a minute, return the chops to the pan and simmer them 10 minutes longer over the lowest possible flame. Add 1 tablespoon of Madeira 2 or 3 minutes before serving. Serves four.

71

THE IDYLLIC CHÂTEAU—AZAY-LE-RIDEAU *Touraine*

Flambééd Bananas

Bananes Flambées

(Bananas, lemon juice, butter, sugar, brandy or orange Curaçao)

Peel 8 ripe bananas and remove the strings. Arrange the bananas close together in a shallow baking dish, add 4 tablespoons of water and sprinkle the bananas with 4 teaspoons of lemon juice. Put several dots of butter and 1 tablespoon of sugar on each banana. Bake them in a 400° oven, basting once or twice and adding a little water if necessary. In 20 minutes the bananas should be soft and beginning to glaze. Bring a pony of warmed brandy or orange Curaçao and the bananas, piping hot, to the table. Put a match to the liqueur, pour it flaming over the bananas and shake the dish gently until the flame dies. Serves six.

72

LATE AFTERNOON IN OLD MENTON

Riviera Pizza

Pissaladière

(Hot roll or French bread dough, onions, garlic, olive oil, anchovies, black olives)

A *pissaladière* should be made with French bread dough (see *Index*), but a standard American hot roll mix will do very nicely. Line an oiled cookie sheet with a layer of dough ⅛ inch thick and roll the edges to make a border. In an iron skillet over a low flame cook 3 pounds of sliced onions and 2 minced cloves of garlic in 1 cup of olive oil until they are quite soft. Drain the onions well, cool them and spread them evenly over the dough. Make a lattice work of anchovy fillets, not too close together, over the onions and in each square place a pitted black Italian olive. Bake the *pissaladière* in a 350° oven for 20 minutes, or until the edges of the crust are brown, and serve it hot.

D

SHEPHERD WITH HIS FLOCK — PACY-SUR-EURE   *Normandy*

Lamb Stew

Navarin de Mouton

(Stewing lamb, onions, garlic, herbs, white wine, stock, carrots, potatoes, turnips)

In a deep casserole brown together 1½ pounds of good lean stewing lamb, cut in cubes, 1 chopped onion and 6 small whole onions in 2 or 3 tablespoons of oil or lard. Pour off any excess fat and sprinkle the lamb with 1 tablespoon of flour. Blend in the flour and add salt and pepper, 1 minced clove of garlic, a *bouquet garni*, ½ cup of white wine, 1 cup of veal stock or chicken consommé, and just enough hot water to cover. Cover the casserole and simmer the stew over the lowest possible flame for 1½ hours. Add 2 carrots, 2 small white turnips and 2 potatoes, all cut in pieces. Simmer the *navarin* for another ½ hour, or until the meat and vegetables are all tender. Serves four.

ROQUEFORT HILLSIDE   *Guyenne*

Epicures' Canapés

Diablotins d'Epicures

(Roquefort cheese, butter, walnut meats, red pepper, French bread)

These are hot hors-d'oeuvre of generous proportions, intended for hungry and appreciative guests and not for mere nibblers.

Cream together to a smooth paste 1 cup of crumbled Roquefort cheese and ¼ pound of butter. Mix in thoroughly ½ cup of finely chopped walnut meats and a pinch of red pepper. Toast slices of French bread on one side, spread the cheese mixture on the untoasted side and brown the *diablotins* briefly in a hot oven.

75

HILLSIDE VILLAGE — ST. ROME-DE-CERNAN *Gascony*

Vermicelli and Onion Soup

Tourin des Landes

(Onions, butter, bacon fat, vermicelli, tomato paste, stock or consommé, Parmesan)

In a heavy casserole or saucepan sauté 4 chopped onions in 1 tablespoon each of butter and bacon fat until they are soft and just beginning to brown. Stir in ¾ cup of fine vermicelli, broken in pieces, and let them take on a little color. Blend in 3 tablespoons of tomato paste and add 6 cups of good beef or chicken stock or consommé. Simmer the soup for 10 minutes and serve it with grated Parmesan. Serves six.

76

THE CHÂTEAU — LUNÉVILLE

Lorraine

Baked Whole Liver

Foie de Veau Bourgeoise

(Calf's liver, salt pork, brandy, herbs, spices, onions, carrots, white wine, egg yolk)

This splendid dish does require time and trouble, but it is a masterpiece. If any is left over it will be delectable cold, served as a pâté.

Moisten 4 ounces of salt pork, cut in long thin strips, with a little brandy. Roll the strips in a mixture of minced parsley, pepper and a pinch each of powdered cinnamon and clove. With a larding needle run the seasoned salt pork through a small whole calf's liver (about 3 pounds). Marinate the liver for 4 hours, in a covered bowl just big enough to hold it, with 3 tablespoons of olive oil, the juice of ½ a lemon, salt, pepper and a little more cinnamon and clove.

Melt 2 tablespoons of butter in a heavy casserole, add the liver, the marinade, 1 onion and 1 carrot, both cut in small pieces, and a *bouquet garni*. Bake the liver, covered, in a 350° oven for 45 minutes, basting it often. Then add a *garniture bourgeoise* (see *Index*) and bake it for another 15 minutes. Remove the liver to a hot platter and surround it with the *garniture*. Add ½ cup of dry white wine to the juice in the casserole, simmer the sauce for 5 minutes and strain it into a small saucepan. Mix a spoonful of the sauce with 1 beaten egg yolk, slowly stir the egg mixture into the sauce, reheat it, stirring constantly, until it just begins to thicken and pour it over the liver. Serves six to eight.

77

THE PONT DU GARD, NEAR NÎMES   *Languedoc*

Spiced Onion Hors-d'Oeuvre

Oignons à la Grecque

(Onions, consommé, vinegar, raisins, tomato paste, herbs, spices)

In a skillet brown 1½ pounds of very small white onions on all sides in 2 tablespoons of butter. In a saucepan combine ¾ cup of strong consommé, ¼ cup wine vinegar, ¾ cup of seedless raisins, 3 tablespoons of tomato paste, 1 tablespoon of salad oil, 2 tablespoons of sugar, ½ teaspoon salt, ⅛ teaspoon of crushed red pepper, ¼ teaspoon of dried thyme, 1 bay leaf and a generous grinding of black pepper. Simmer this sauce for 2 or 3 minutes. Arrange the browned onions close together in a shallow baking dish and cover them with the sauce. Bake them in a 325° oven for 1 hour, or until they are tender when pricked with a fork. Serve *oignons à la grecque* chilled, as an hors-d'oeuvre or with cold meats.

78

THE WALLS OF THE CITE — CARCASSONNE *Languedoc*

Veal Scallops with Tarragon

Escalopes de Veau à l'Estragon

(Veal scallops, consommé, tomato paste, tarragon)

Use 4 large veal scallops cut very thin and pounded even thinner with a wooden mallet or potato masher. Salt and pepper the scallops and dip them lightly in flour. Sauté them in an iron skillet over a medium flame with 2 tablespoons of hot butter until they are brown on each side. Put the scallops on a platter and keep them hot. Stir ½ cup of consommé or juices from a roast, 1 tablespoon of tomato paste and 1 teaspoon of chopped fresh tarragon into the pan juices. Simmer the sauce for 2 or 3 minutes and pour it over the scallops. If you use dried tarragon, it will have more flavor if it is soaked in a few drops of hot water before it is added to the sauce. Serves four.

79

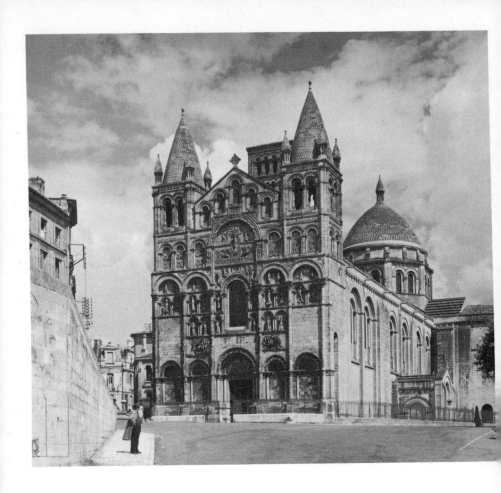

CATHEDRAL OF ST. PIERRE—ANGOULÊME   *Angoumois*

Pork Chops and Baby Turnips
Côtelettes de Porc aux Navets

(Pork chops, butter, small blue-nose turnips, white wine, parsley)

In a large heavy skillet brown well-trimmed pork chops on both sides in butter. For each chop add 1 young blue-nose turnip, peeled and quartered, and 2 or 3 tablespoons of white wine or chicken consommé, and season with salt and pepper. Cover the skillet, lower the flame, and cook the chops and turnips together, shaking the pan occasionally, for 40 minutes, or until the turnips are tender and browned on all sides. Serve sprinkled with chopped parsley.

DETAIL OF THE CATHEDRAL PORCH—BOURGES   *Berry*

Sausages in White Wine Sauce

Saucisses au Vin Blanc

(Country sausage, butter, shallot, herbs, white wine)

Use fresh pork sausages of the kind generally known as country sausage. Brown
the sausages slowly in a skillet, pricking the skins first so they will not burst.
Remove the sausages when they are done and drain them on brown paper. Pour
off all the fat in the skillet. For 1 pound of sausages (enough to serve 3 or 4),
melt 1 tablespoon of butter in the skillet and add 1 minced shallot. Sauté the
shallot for about 30 seconds, then blend in ½ tablespoon of flour and cook the
mixture for 2 or 3 minutes. Then add a *bouquet garni* and 1½ cups of dry white
wine, and simmer the sauce for 20 minutes. Remove the *bouquet*, return the
sausages to the skillet and reheat them in the sauce. Serve with mashed potatoes.

D   81

HEMING, A FARM VILLAGE IN THE ARDENNES   *Champagne*

Ardennes Stuffed Baked Potatoes

Pommes de Terre à l'Ardennaise

(Potatoes, cream, egg yolks, butter, grated cheese, nutmeg, parsley, mushrooms)

Slit the tops of 6 baked Idaho potatoes lengthwise and scoop out the pulp. Mash the potato and beat in 2 tablespoons of butter, ¾ cup cream mixed with 3 egg yolks, and 2 tablespoons of grated Parmesan. Add salt and pepper to taste, a pinch of nutmeg and 1 tablespoon of minced parsley. Parboil 6 mushrooms in salted water for 4 or 5 minutes, drain them, chop them finely and add them to the potatoes. Stuff the potato skins with this delicious purée, sprinkle them with more grated Parmesan, dot them with butter, and return them to a 350° oven for 15 minutes, or until the cheese is lightly browned. Serves six.

THE CHURCH OF NOTRE-DAME-DE-L'ÉPINE *Champagne*

Fresh-water Fisherman's Stew
Matelote Champenoise
(Fresh-water fish, shallots, garlic, spices, herbs, white wine, brandy)

This dish from the Champagne country is a stand-by of the vacationing angler. The more fish you catch for it yourself, the better it will taste.

Melt 4 tablespoons of butter in a large saucepan and add 3 shallots and 2 cloves of garlic, all minced, salt, freshly ground black pepper, a pinch of cinnamon, 2 cloves and a *bouquet garni*. When the butter is hot, add 4 pounds of cleaned fresh-water fish cut in 1½-inch slices. Eel is essential and the others may be pickerel, pike, carp, trout or whitefish. Whatever the selection you have available, use roughly equal quantities of each kind of fish. Heat the fish in the butter for several minutes, then add 3 cups of dry white wine, cover the saucepan and cook the *matelote* over a fairly brisk flame for 20 minutes.

Warm a tablespoon of brandy, put a match to it and pour it flaming over the fish stew. When the flame dies, ladle the fish into a deep serving dish and remove the *bouquet garni*. Add a tablespoon of butter creamed with a teaspoon of flour to the sauce, and let it simmer and thicken slightly for a few minutes. Pour the sauce over the fish and garnish the *matelote* with chopped parsley and slices of French bread sautéed in butter until they are crisp and golden. Serves six.

83

FLANDERS FIELDS NEAR CALAIS   *Flanders*

Flemish Red Cabbage and Apples

Choux Rouges à la Flamande

(Red cabbage, onion, bacon fat, apples, red wine, sugar, spices)

Soak 4 cups of finely shredded red cabbage in cold water for 1 hour and drain it. Chop 2 medium onions and sauté them in a heavy saucepan in 2 tablespoons of bacon fat until they are golden. Add 2 tart apples, peeled, cored and sliced, and simmer together for 5 minutes. Then add the cabbage, 2 tablespoons of brown sugar, salt, pepper and a pinch of either powdered clove or nutmeg. Add ½ cup each of water and red wine, cover the pan, and simmer the cabbage gently until it is very tender, or for at least 1 hour. Add a little red wine if the liquid cooks away too fast. Serves four to six.

VINEYARDS AT VERZENAY *Champagne*

Spinach Purée with Stuffed Eggs

Epinards à la Chimay

(Spinach, eggs, onion, shallot, mushrooms, butter, cream, nutmeg)

Simmer 1 small onion, 1 small shallot and 4 large mushrooms, all finely minced, in 1 tablespoon of butter until they are soft and reduced. Season with salt, pepper and grated nutmeg. Cut 6 hard-boiled eggs in half lengthwise; remove the yolks and mash them with the mushroom mixture, 2 teaspoons of butter, a little cream and a touch of cayenne. Stuff the egg whites with the yolk mixture, sprinkle them lightly with fine bread crumbs, and dot them with butter.

Meanwhile, in a covered kettle cook 3 pounds of spinach with ½ cup of water for 10 minutes, or until it is just soft, and purée it in an electric blender. Reheat the spinach over a good flame to cook away all excess liquid, then add a lump of butter, ⅓ cup of extra-heavy cream or sour cream, and salt and pepper. Brown the stuffed eggs lightly under the broiler; put the spinach purée in a deep serving dish, arrange the eggs in a circle on top and serve immediately. Serves six.

THE PRÉFECTURE OF THE OISE — BEAUVAIS   *Ile-de-France*

Roast Tenderloin of Beef Jardinière
Filet de Boeuf Jardinière
(Tenderloin of beef, beef stock or consommé, garden vegetables)

This is a perfectionist's dish. Not complicated, just perfect. The *jardinière* is a panorama of tiny vegetables with which only your own *jardin* or a green-grocer with an exceptional conscience can supply you.

Salt and pepper a tenderloin of beef (about 3½ pounds), tie a thin layer of salt pork over it and roast it in a 350° oven for 50 minutes, basting it frequently. Remove the salt pork and put the roast on a large, hot platter. Skim the excess fat from the pan juices, stir in briskly a little hot beef stock or consommé and serve the juice in a sauceboat.

Around the roast arrange alternating piles of the smallest possible garden vegetables: carrots and blue-nose turnips cooked separately in beef stock or consommé; green peas cooked in a minimum of water with a few lettuce leaves and a small onion; green beans cooked in a minimum of water and sprinkled with minced parsley; and instead of potatoes, white shell beans boiled until tender but not broken and also sprinkled with parsley. Pour a little melted butter on all the vegetables. The final touch of perfection, if you still have the patience, would be flowerettes of steamed cauliflower for which a sauceboat of hollandaise sauce should come separately to the table.

MONDAY ON THE OLD CANAL — STRASBOURG   *Alsace*

Alsatian Sauerkraut
Choucroute Garnie Alsacienne
(Sauerkraut, white wine, spices, bacon, frankfurters, ham, potatoes)

Canned sauerkraut is excellent for this, but it will need a little doctoring. Use a standard can, or about 1¾ pounds. Wash the sauerkraut thoroughly in cold water, drain it and press out the excess liquid. Put it in a heavy saucepan, tightly covered, with 1 cup of dry white wine, 2 tablespoons of vinegar, 20 juniper berries, 10 whole peppercorns and ½ pound of lean bacon, cut in chunks. Cook the sauerkraut over the lowest possible flame for 1¼ hours, or until most of the liquid is absorbed. Ten minutes before servingtime, prick the skins of 6 frankfurters or *knackwurst* with a fork and add them and 6 generous slices of baked ham to the sauerkraut. Heat the *choucroute* thoroughly, still covered; then pile the sauerkraut in the center of a large platter, cover it neatly with the ham and surround it with the sausages, the pieces of bacon and 6 boiled potatoes. Serve with a pot of strong mustard. Serves six.

CHÂTEAU DE VALENÇAY   *Touraine*

French Butter Cookies

Sablés

(Flour, sugar, salt, egg yolk, ice water, vanilla, butter)

From their short and granular texture, the name *sablé*, or "sandy," was coined for these traditional cookies:

Sift together into a bowl 1¼ cups of flour, 4 tablespoons of sugar, and a pinch of salt, and make a well in the center. Into the well put 1 egg yolk, 1 tablespoon of ice water, ½ teaspoon of vanilla extract, and 6½ tablespoons of butter, cold and cut into small bits. With the fingers quickly work the butter into the liquids and gradually draw in the flour, mixing the pastry as fast as possible so as not to warm the butter. Sprinkle on a little more flour if necessary, until the dough just holds together and is not sticky. Gather it together into a ball, put it in a floured bowl, and let it stand for ½ hour in the refrigerator. Then roll it out quickly on a floured board to a thickness of a little less than ¼ inch. Cut it into circles with a 2½-inch scalloped cooky cutter and bake the *sablés* on a buttered cooky sheet in a preheated 350° oven for 18 minutes, or until they are cooked through but pale gold, not brown. Cool on a cake rack.

MARTIGUES, "THE VENICE OF PROVENCE"   *Provence*

Eggplant and Tomato Ragout
Ratatouille
(Eggplant, tomatoes, onions, peppers, zucchini, oil, garlic, herbs)

Peel a medium eggplant and cut it in slices ½ inch thick. Salt the slices lightly, pile them together and let them stand under a weight for ½ hour. In a large skillet, over a low flame, sauté 2 large sliced onions and 2 diced green peppers, or sweet red ones, in ½ cup of olive oil. When the vegetables begin to soften, add 4 ripe tomatoes, peeled, seeded and coarsely chopped, the slices of eggplant, drained and cut into dice, and 2 zucchini, cut in ½-inch slices. Add salt and pepper, 1 tablespoon of chopped parsley, and a pinch each of marjoram and basil. Simmer the *ratatouille* for about 45 minutes, or until the vegetables are all soft and the liquid is quite reduced, but be careful not to let them cook to a purée. About 15 minutes before the *ratatouille* is ready, add 1 small minced and crushed clove of garlic. Serves four as a hot vegetable, eight or more as a cold hors-d'oeuvre.

THE VILLAGE AT NOONTIME — EVRY-LES-CHÂTEAUX   *Ile-de-France*

Calves' Brains with Black Butter

Cervelles au Beurre Noir

(Calves' brains, butter, vinegar, capers)

Soak 4 calves' brains in cold water for 1 hour. Drain them, remove the outer membranes, rinse the brains and drop them into boiling water with a little lemon juice and salt. Simmer them for 15 minutes, drain them again and let them stand covered with ice water until they are thoroughly cooled. Dry the brains with a towel and dip them in a little flour seasoned with salt and pepper. In a skillet sauté them gently in butter until they are lightly browned on all sides and remove them to a heated platter. Add 6 tablespoons of butter to the skillet and when it takes on a nut-brown color take the skillet off the fire and stir in 1 tablespoon of vinegar. Heat the mixture until it foams and add 4 teaspoons of drained capers. Pour this *beurre noir* over the brains and serve immediately. Serves four.

THE RIVER TARN — MONTAUBAN   *Guyenne*

Sautéed Lobster Cettoise

Homard à la Cettoise

(Lobster, onion, olive oil, garlic, ham, parsley, tomato paste, stock, egg yolk)

Split a 2-pound live lobster down the center and cut it in thick pieces, shell and all, discarding the head. This is not as hard as it sounds, but have someone at the fish market do it for you if you'd rather. In a heavy skillet sauté 1 medium onion, chopped, in 3 tablespoons of olive oil until it is soft. Add the cut up lobster and turn the pieces to color the shells on all sides. Add 1 clove of garlic, chopped and mashed, 2 tablespoons of chopped ham and 1 tablespoon of minced parsley and sauté everything together over a low flame for 10 minutes. Sprinkle 1 scant tablespoon of flour over the lobster, add 1 heaping tablespoon of tomato paste and blend these thoroughly into the pan juices. Add ¾ cup of chicken stock or consommé and salt and pepper to taste, and simmer the *homard*, covered, for another 10 minutes. Remove it to a deep serving dish and keep it hot. Add a spoonful of the sauce to 1 beaten egg yolk and stir the egg mixture gradually into the sauce. Heat it, stirring constantly, without allowing it to boil and pour it over the lobster. Serves two.

CLOISTER OF THE BENEDICTINE ABBEY — CHARLIEU   *Lyonnais*

Green Beans and Onions

Haricots Verts à la Lyonnaise

(Green beans, onion, wine vinegar, parsley)

Lyons is famous for its wonderful food. Most *lyonnais* recipes have a characteristic savor of sautéed onion.

Snap off the stems and tips of 1 pound of young green beans. Leave the beans whole, boil them in a minimum of salted water until they are tender but still firm, and drain them thoroughly. In a heavy pan sauté 1 chopped onion in 2 tablespoons of butter until it is soft and golden. Add the green beans, mix them well with the onion and butter and reheat them over a low flame for a few minutes. Add salt and pepper to taste and ½ teaspoon of wine vinegar. Sprinkle the beans with finely chopped parsley before serving. Serves four.

THE CHÂTEAU DE CHAMBORD *Orléanais*

Upside-down Apple Tart

Tarte Tatin

(Apples, butter, sugar, pie pastry, whipped cream)

Use a round, glass baking dish about 2 inches deep. Butter it very generously and cover the bottom with a ¼-inch layer of sugar. On the sugar arrange a layer of neatly overlapping slices of tart apples, peeled and cored. Then fill the dish to the top with more sliced apples, sprinkle them with sugar and dot them lavishly with butter. Cover the dish with a circle of flaky pie dough and bake the tart in a 375° oven for about 30 minutes. The tart is ready when the apples are golden and the sugar is beginning to caramelize. Then loosen the crust all the way around, put a serving platter upside down over the baking dish, turn the whole thing over and remove the baking dish. Serve the *tarte Tatin* hot, with chilled whipped cream.

THE LOWER TOWN — SEMUR-EN-AUXOIS   *Burgundy*

Burgundian Beef Stew

Boeuf Bourguignon

(Beef, red wine, onions, carrots, garlic, shallots, veal knuckle, brandy, mushrooms)

Boeuf bourguignon comes from the province of the most fabulous vineyards of France and is a great classic of regional cookery.

In an iron *cocotte* or a heavy casserole brown 2 pounds of good lean stewing beef, cut in 1½-inch cubes, in 2 tablespoons of hot butter. Sprinkle the meat with 1 tablespoon of flour, blend it in thoroughly and add salt and pepper and 1½ cups of red wine. In a small frying pan brown 2 coarsely chopped onions in 1 tablespoon of butter. Add the onions to the meat, together with 1 carrot, cut in pieces, 1 clove of garlic and 2 shallots, all finely chopped, a *bouquet garni,* and a piece of cracked veal knuckle if one is available. Add just enough water to cover the meat, cover the *cocotte* and simmer the stew over a low flame for 3 hours, or until the meat is very tender and the sauce is a rich, dark brown.

Half an hour before servingtime, add 1 tablespoon of brandy, 4 tablespoons of Madeira if you have some, and ½ pound of raw mushroom caps. Remove the *bouquet garni* and serve the *boeuf bourguignon* with buttered rice. Serves four.

VILLAGE ARCADE — LOUHANS   *Bresse*

Madame Blanc's Chicken in Cream
Poulet à la Crème Madame Blanc
(Chicken, onion, heavy cream)

Cut a small chicken into serving pieces. In a heavy skillet over a low flame heat the pieces in 2 tablespoons of hot butter, covered, for 5 minutes, being sure not to let them brown. Sprinkle the pieces with 1 tablespoon of flour, blend it thoroughly into the pan juices and add 1 whole onion, salt and pepper and enough hot water almost to cover the chicken. Cover the skillet and simmer the chicken for 20 to 30 minutes, or until it is tender and the stock is reduced to about 1 cup. Discard the onion, put the chicken in a deep serving platter and keep it hot. Add 1 cup of very heavy cream to the stock, simmer the sauce briefly, taste it for seasoning and pour it over the chicken. This *sauce à la crème* should be plentiful and almost white. Serves four.

MONT BLANC IN SUMMER *Savoy*

Marinated Roast Leg of Lamb

Gigot à la Génoise

(Leg of lamb, oil, white wine, vegetables, anchovies, bacon, herbs, spices)

Remove as much fat and skin as possible from a small leg of lamb. Insert a cut clove of garlic near the bone at each end of the roast and marinate it for 24 hours with ½ cup of oil, ½ cup of white wine, 1 onion and 1 carrot, both sliced, and 4 whole cloves. The next day put the leg of lamb in a roasting pan and over it slice 2 stalks of celery and 2 small sour pickles. Sprinkle it with a little chopped terragon and across the top arrange 4 anchovy filets and 2 strips of bacon. Roast the *gigot* in a 400° oven for 18 minutes per pound, basting it often, until it is done but still pink in the center. Carve it at the table and serve the pan juices, diluted with a little hot water or stock, in a sauceboat. Be sure to skim the excess fat from them first.

BACK GARDENS OF SAINTES   *Saintonge*

Marinated Beef Hors-d'Oeuvre
Salade de Boeuf
(Cooked beef, onions, carrot, French dressing, parsley)

This is a thrifty classic of the French hors-d'oeuvre tray: Cut leftover cooked beef into thin julienne strips and put it in a shallow serving dish. Over the meat scatter very thin slices of small white onions and a few thin circles of raw carrot. Marinate the salad for 2 or 3 hours in a generous amount of French dressing made of 1 part of wine vinegar, 3 parts of olive oil, and salt, pepper and prepared mustard to taste. Sprinkle the *salade de boeuf* with chopped parsley just before serving.

THE INLET — ST. VALERY-SUR-SOMME   *Picardy*

Baked Eggs in Tomatoes

Oeufs aux Pommes d'Amour

(Tomatoes, parsley, garlic, eggs, cheese, bread crumbs)

Cut a slice from the stem ends of ripe tomatoes, shake out the seeds and scoop out some of the pulp. Sauté the tomatoes, cut side up, in a little olive oil for 3 or 4 minutes. Transfer them carefully to a shallow baking dish and sprinkle them with chopped parsley and a little chopped and mashed garlic. Break an egg into each tomato and sprinkle them with salt, pepper, grated Swiss cheese, bread crumbs and a little melted butter. Bake the *pommes d'amour* in a 400° oven for 10 minutes, or until the eggs are set and the crumbs are lightly browned.

ROMANESQUE REMNANTS — CHAUVIGNY   *Poitou*

Poached Eggs Saint-Germain
Oeufs Pochés Saint-Germain

(Purée of split green peas, eggs, cream sauce, Swiss cheese, butter)

The traditional ingredient in any dish called *Saint-Germain* is a purée of green peas, either dried or fresh ones.

Spread a ½-inch layer of hot purée of green peas in a shallow baking dish. Poach 4 eggs and arrange them on the purée. Over the eggs pour a cream sauce made with 1 tablespoon of butter melted and blended with 1 teaspoon of flour, 1 cup of cream, stirred in gradually, salt and pepper and 2 tablespoons of grated Swiss cheese. Pour a little melted butter over the sauce and glaze the *oeufs pochés* briefly under a hot broiler. Serves four.

99

THE BUSY HARBOR — MARSEILLES   *Provence*

Mackerel with Olives

Maquereaux aux Olives

(Mackerel, green olives, black olives, lemon)

Grease the bottom of a shallow glass or earthenware baking dish with a little salad oil. Choose small fresh mackerel, allowing one per person, and stuff each one with 5 or 6 small pitted green olives. Arrange the fish in the baking dish, sprinkle them with a little more oil and with salt and freshly ground black pepper. Scatter a handful of small black Italian or Greek olives around the fish and bake the *maquereaux aux olives* in a 350° oven for about 25 minutes. Garnish the mackerel with circles of lemon and serve them from the baking dish.

PROVENÇAL FARMHOUSES — LES BAUX   *Provence*

Provençal Tomatoes

Tomates Provençale

(Tomatoes, olive oil, garlic, parsley, bread crumbs)

Cut 4 large, red tomatoes in half, shake out the seeds, and season with salt and pepper. In an iron skillet cook the tomatoes lightly on both sides in 4 tablespoons of hot olive oil. Add 2 minced cloves of garlic and cook the tomatoes another 2 or 3 minutes. Remove them to a heated platter and sprinkle them plentifully with chopped parsley. Add 2 heaping tablespoons of coarse bread crumbs to the oil remaining in the skillet, sauté them for a minute or two until they are brown and have absorbed the oil, and sprinkle them over the tomatoes. Serves four.

101

THE ARCADED FARM — ST. CYR-SUR-MENTHON *Bresse*

Pumpkin Soup

Soupe au Potiron

(Pumpkin, onion, milk, cream, eggs, butter)

Cut 1 pound of pumpkin into pieces, peel them and put them in a soup kettle with 1 sliced onion and 6 cups of salted water. Cover the kettle and boil the pumpkin for 15 minutes, or until it is soft. Drain off the water and reserve it, and force the pumpkin through a sieve. Put this purée in the top of a double boiler and add 1¾ cups of milk and ¼ cup of cream. *Soupe au potiron* should be quite rich and thick, but you will probably still need to dilute the pumpkin and milk mixture with some of the reserved cooking water. Add salt and pepper to taste and cook the soup over simmering water for 20 minutes.

Mix a few spoonfuls of soup with 2 beaten eggs. Add the egg mixture gradually to the soup, stirring constantly, and keep stirring until it begins to thicken. Then stir in a lump of butter and serve immediately. Serves four.

HILLSIDE HABITATIONS — ROC-AMADOUR *Guyenne*

Veal Chops en Cocotte

Côtes de Veau en Cocotte

(Veal chops, onions, new potatoes, mushrooms)

In an iron skillet sauté a dozen very small whole onions in hot butter. When they are brown, add a little water, salt and pepper, and 1 teaspoon of sugar. Simmer the onions, covered, until they are almost cooked through and the water is absorbed. Scrape and wipe dry 16 small new potatoes. Sauté them very slowly in another skillet, uncovered, in plenty of butter, tossing them often. They should brown gradually and cook through at the same time.

Meanwhile, in an iron *cocotte* or a heavy casserole brown 4 veal chops quickly on both sides in 3 tablespoons of butter. Lower the flame, cover the *cocotte* and simmer the chops gently for about 20 minutes. When they are almost done, add the onions, ¼ pound of quartered raw mushrooms, salt and pepper if necessary, and 3 or 4 tablespoons of consommé. Simmer the chops and vegetables together, uncovered, for 5 to 10 minutes. Add the potatoes and sprinkle the dish with chopped parsley before serving. Serves four.

VIEUX PALAIS—ESPALION *Guyenne*

Baked Fillet of Sole Gironde

Sole Gratinée comme en Gironde

(Fillets of sole, mushrooms, shallots, herbs, bread crumbs, white wine, stock)

Butter a shallow baking dish with 1 tablespoon of butter creamed with 1 teaspoon of flour. Mix together ¼ pound of mushrooms and 2 shallots, all finely chopped, 1 teaspoon of minced chives, and 1 tablespoon of minced parsley. Spread half this mixture in the baking dish, sprinkle it lightly with fine bread crumbs, and arrange 8 fillets of sole or flounder on top. Cover the fish with the rest of the chopped vegetables, sprinkle lightly again with bread crumbs and with a little grated Swiss cheese, and dot with butter. Add ½ cup each of white wine and chicken stock or consommé, and bake the fish in a moderate oven for 20 to 25 minutes. Serves four.

THE CHÂTEAU OF MADAME DE MAINTENON *Orléanais*

Lamb Kidneys de Latour
Rognons de Mouton de Latour

(Kidneys, onion, butter, flour, beef stock, vinegar, mustard, shallot or garlic)

Soak 12 lamb kidneys in cold water for 20 minutes. Remove the skins, split the kidneys lengthwise with a sharp knife, removing the central gristle, and arrange them in a shallow pan for broiling. Prepare the following sauce first, then broil the kidneys under a brisk flame for about 10 minutes, turning them often.

In a small heavy saucepan sauté 1 tablespoon of minced onion in 2 tablespoons of butter until the onion is soft. Blend in 1½ teaspoons of flour and let the mixture thicken slightly and take on a little color. Add 1¼ cups of beef stock or consommé, 2 teaspoons of wine vinegar, 1 teaspoon of mild prepared mustard, and 1 small minced shallot or clove of garlic. Season with salt and pepper and let the sauce simmer very slowly for 20 minutes. When the kidneys are done, transfer them to a hot platter and strain the sauce over them. Serves four to six.

THE FORTIFIED HARBOR — LA ROCHELLE   *Aunis*

Artichoke and Shrimp Hors-d'Oeuvre
Fonds d'Artichauts aux Crevettes
(Artichokes, oil, vinegar, shrimp, green pepper, mayonnaise, lemon juice, paprika)

Boil 6 artichokes in salted water for 45 minutes or until the bases are tender when pricked with a sharp knife. Drain them and remove the leaves and chokes. Marinate the bases for 1 hour in 3 tablespoons of salad oil, 1½ tablespoons of wine vinegar and salt and pepper. Mix 1 cup of cooked shrimp, cut in small pieces, with ½ a finely diced green pepper and ⅓ cup of mayonnaise seasoned with lemon, freshly ground pepper and paprika. Fill the artichoke bases with the shrimp mixture, mask them with a very thin layer of mayonnaise and decorate each one with half a whole shrimp, split lengthwise, and a tiny sprig of parsley. Chill thoroughly. Serves six.

106

PLACE DU PALAIS — RENNES   *Brittany*

Chocolate Mousse

Mousse au Chocolat

(Bittersweet chocolate, vanilla, eggs)

Over simmering water in the top of a double boiler melt ½ pound of bittersweet chocolate, broken in pieces, with ¼ cup of water. Stir the chocolate until
it is smooth and set it aside to cool. Then add 5 egg yolks beaten with 1 teaspoon
of vanilla extract. Transfer the mixture to a bowl and carefully but thoroughly
fold in 5 stiffly beaten egg whites. Fill small individual ramekins or *pots de crème*
with the mousse and chill for at least 2 hours before serving. Serves six.

COUNTRY ROAD IN THE FINISTÈRE   *Brittany*

Split-Pea Soup
Purée Saint-Germain
(Split peas, bacon, beef consommé, herbs, croutons)

Soak 1 pound of green split peas for 4 hours. Drain them and cook them, covered, in 4 cups of salted water, skimming once or twice, until they are soft. Drain the peas again, reserving the cooking water, and force them through a sieve. In a heavy saucepan sauté 3 tablespoons of finely minced fat bacon. Add the cooking water, 1½ cups of beef consommé or stock, the puréed peas and a *bouquet garni.* Simmer the soup for 15 minutes, remove the *bouquet garni,* stir in 1 tablespoon of butter creamed with 1 teaspoon of flour, and serve the *purée Saint-Germain* with a sprinkling of crisp brown croutons sautéed in butter. Serves six to eight.

108

PORCH OF THE CATHEDRAL—AMIENS *Picardy*

Poached Salmon with Green Mayonnaise

Saumon Poché, Sauce Verte

(Salmon, herbs, sour cream, homemade mayonnaise, tomatoes, cucumbers)

In 2 quarts of water simmer for 15 minutes 1 carrot and 1 onion, both cut in pieces, 2 sprigs of parsley, 1 bay leaf, ½ teaspoon of thyme, ½ dozen pepper corns, 1 tablespoon of salt and ½ cup of white wine. Then put in a 3-pound piece of salmon wrapped in a square of cheese cloth. When the liquid returns to the boil, turn the flame very low and poach the salmon, covered, for 25 minutes. Remove the cover and cool the fish in the cooking liquid; then drain and unwrap it, chill it and skin the top side before masking it with the following *sauce verte:*

Trim the stems from fresh spinach, water cress, parsley and tarragon. Measure, quite firmly packed, 1 cup of spinach, ½ cup of water cress, ½ cup of parsley and ¼ cup of tarragon. Drop all these greens into boiling water and let them boil for 3 minutes, uncovered. Turn them into a sieve, cool them under running water, and squeeze them dry in a cloth. Chop them as finely as possible, add about ¼ cup of sour cream and reduce them to a fine purée in an electric blender. Mix the green purée thoroughly with 1½ cups of homemade mayonnaise; use part of this sauce to mask the salmon and serve the rest in a sauceboat. Garnish the platter with water cress and with peeled, hollowed and well-drained tomatoes stuffed with diced cucumbers seasoned with French dressing and minced parsley.

MEDITERRANEAN AFTERNOON — ANTIBES *Riviera*

Baked Zucchini

Zucchini au Four

(Zucchini, shallots, bread crumbs, bacon)

Split 6 small zucchini lengthwise and parboil them in salted water for 5 minutes. Drain them, arrange them, skin side down, in a shallow baking dish and sprinkle them lightly with 6 minced shallots, bread crumbs and salt and pepper. Dot them with butter and put a strip of bacon on each one. Bake the zucchini in a 350° oven for about 30 minutes, or until they are tender and the bacon is brown. Serves four to six.

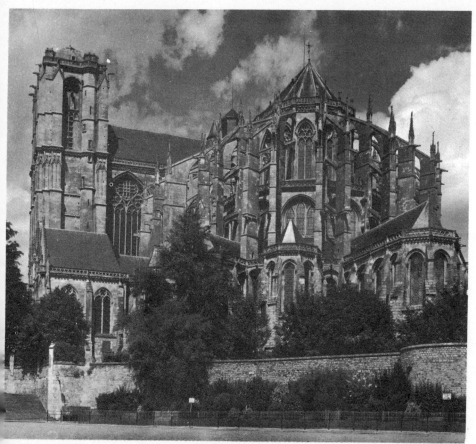

CATHÉDRALE ST. JULIEN — LE MANS   *Maine*

Mushrooms in Cream

Champignons à la Crème

(Mushrooms, onion, butter, heavy cream)

This is an epicure's dish for the season when the finest fresh mushrooms are in the markets.

In an iron skillet sauté 1 small minced onion in 2 tablespoons of butter until it is soft but not brown. Add 1 pound of fresh mushrooms, sliced, and cook them over a medium flame until most of the liquid has evaporated. Season them with salt and pepper and blend in 1 teaspoon of flour. Add ¾ cup of warm, heavy cream and simmer the *champignons à la crème* for 2 or 3 minutes, or until the sauce thickens slightly. Serve them on buttered toast or with rice. Serves four.

111

CHAPEL OF STE. CROIX—ABBAYE DE MONTMAJOUR   *Provence*

Steamed Salt Cod with Garlic Mayonnaise

Aïoli Provençal

(Salt cod, vegetables, garlic mayonnaise)

The *aïoli* is a pungent Mediterranean mayonnaise which is served in large quantities, thoroughly chilled, with hot, steamed salt cod fillets, hard-boiled eggs and boiled vegetables; whole new potatoes in their jackets, small whole artichokes, leeks with the green tops trimmed off, and carrots and blue-nose turnips, cut in pieces, are the usual assortment.

Use as many cloves of garlic in the *aïoli* as you dare. The correct recipe calls for 8 cloves per cup of homemade mayonnaise; 3 cloves is about the minimum if the dish is to keep its character. Start with the garlic, minced and mashed to a pulp, in a bowl. With a sauce whisk beat in 2 egg yolks. Add ¼ teaspoon of salt and a little freshly ground pepper; then add, drop by drop, 4 tablespoons of chilled olive oil, stirring furiously. Pour this mixture into an electric blender, turn the blender on and slowly add the juice of ½ a lemon and 1 tablespoon of lukewarm water. Then add gradually 1 cup of chilled olive oil. Do not make more than one cup of *aïoli* at a time in an electric blender.

MANOIR AT OUILLY-LE-TESSON *Normandy*

Eggs Poached in Cream

Oeufs Cocotte à la Crème

(Eggs, butter, heavy cream)

For each egg use a small ovenproof custard cup. Put a small piece of butter in the bottom of each cup, break an egg over the butter and add 2 teaspoons of very heavy cream. Sprinkle lightly with salt and freshly ground black pepper or paprika. Put the custard cups in a large shallow pan and carefully fill the pan with boiling water just to the level of the cream in the cups. Cover the pan, keep the water barely simmering on the top of the stove and cook the eggs for about 6 minutes, or until the whites are set. Test the edges of the *oeufs cocotte* with a spoon before serving as the cooking time depends somewhat on the thickness of the custard cups.

E 113

STILL WATERS — ST. JEAN-PIED-DE-PORT   *Béarn*

Duck with Orange Sauce

Caneton à l'Orange

(Duck, oranges, lemon, vinegar, sugar, liqueur, chicken stock or consommé)

Roast a duck in a 325° oven for 20 to 25 minutes per pound. Prick the skin several times to release the fat and baste the duck often.

Meanwhile grate coarsely the rind of 2 oranges and 1 lemon. Blanch the rind in boiling water for 20 seconds and drain it. In a small saucepan simmer 3 tablespoons of vinegar with 1 tablespoon of sugar until the mixture begins to caramelize. Add the juice of the 2 oranges and the lemon, simmer together briefly and add the blanched rinds. When the duck is done, remove it to a hot platter and decorate it with thin slices of orange, peeled and halved. Skim all the excess fat from the pan juices. Pour in 2 tablespoons of Cointreau or brandy and ¼ cup of hot chicken stock or consommé and scrape in all the brown glaze around the pan. Add this juice to the orange sauce, reheat it, and serve it in a sauceboat.

114

LOW TIDE AT DOUARNENEZ *Brittany*

Stuffed Crab Armoricaine
Crabe Armoricaine

(Crab meat, onion, mushrooms, brandy, tomato paste, curry powder, bread crumbs)

Crabe armoricaine may be served in individual ramekins, but the Bretons serve it more picturesquely in real crab shells.

Chop 1 small onion and ¼ pound of mushrooms and sauté them gently in 1 tablespoon of butter until the onions are soft. Add 1 tablespoon of brandy, 3 tablespoons of tomato paste, ½ teaspoon of curry powder and a pinch each of salt and pepper. Simmer the vegetables for 3 more minutes. If the mixture is very thick, dilute it with a little water or white wine. Add ¾ pound of cooked crab meat, stir the mixture well and stuff 6 crab shells with it. Sprinkle the stuffed shells with fine bread crumbs, dot them with butter and brown them lightly under a hot broiler. Serves six.

THE TOWN GATE — AMMERSCHWIHR   *Alsace*

Alsatian Garlic Potatoes
Pommes de Terre Alsacienne

(Potatoes, eggs, garlic, parsley, nutmeg)

Mash 2 pounds of boiled potatoes and beat in 2 tablespoons of butter and
2 beaten eggs. Mix in thoroughly 2 tablespoons of flour, 2 or 3 minced and crushed
cloves of garlic, 2 tablespoons of very finely chopped parsley, a pinch of nutmeg
and salt and pepper to taste. Transfer the potatoes to a buttered baking dish and
bake them in a 350° oven for 15 minutes, or until the top is lightly browned.
Pour a little melted butter over the crust before serving. Serves four.

ARC DE TRIOMPHE DU CARROUSEL   *Paris*

Roast of Veal Bourgeoise
Rôti de Veau Bourgeoise
(Veal, onions, carrots, white wine, bacon, herbs, stock or consommé)

In an iron casserole or *cocotte* brown a 3½-pound piece of young veal in 2 tablespoons of butter. Add 1 carrot and 1 onion, both cut in pieces, ½ cup of white wine, ¼ cup of water, a *bouquet garni,* salt and pepper, a piece of bacon rind, and ½ teaspoon of meat glaze. Bake the roast, covered, in a 300° oven for 1½ hours, then uncover it and bake it another 30 minutes to brown the meat and reduce the sauce. Serve the *rôti de veau* sliced on a hot platter with the sauce and surrounded by the following *garniture bourgeoise:*

In a skillet sauté 3 strips of lean bacon, diced, in 1 tablespoon of butter. Add a dozen very small onions and, when these are lightly browned on all sides, add 6 young carrots cut in small pieces, salt, pepper, and 1 teaspoon of sugar. When the carrots begin to brown, add 1 cup of beef stock or consommé and simmer the vegetables, covered, until they are tender and very little liquid remains. Serves six to eight.

CHÂTEAU DE MENTHON, NEAR ANNECY   *Savoy*

Chicken Livers Marianne
Foies de Volailles Marianne
(Chicken livers, shallot, red wine, consommé, mushrooms, bacon)

Cut a dozen fresh chicken livers in half. In an iron skillet sauté the pieces briefly in 2 tablespoons of hot butter and remove them while they are still quite pink in the center. To the butter left in the skillet add 1 shallot, minced, and ½ cup of dry red wine. Simmer the liquid down to about one half its original quantity, add ½ cup of consommé and simmer the sauce again for 5 or 6 minutes.

Meanwhile, sauté a dozen small mushroom caps in 1 tablespoon of butter for 3 minutes and blanch ½ cup of very finely diced bacon in boiling water. Drain the bacon and add the mushrooms, bacon and a little freshly ground black pepper to the red wine sauce. Add a little salt if necessary, add the chicken livers, and reheat all together thoroughly. Sprinkle the *foies de volailles Marianne* with chopped parsley and serve them with buttered rice. Serves four.

118

THE CHÂTEAU DE TANLAY   *Burgundy*

Sliced Steak with White Wine Sauce

Steak Morvandiau

(Steak, shallots, mustard, white wine, parsley)

For a thick, rare and juicy steak (about 2 pounds for 4 people) here is a simple sauce in the best tradition of French cooking.

In an iron skillet over a low flame sauté 2 minced shallots in 1 tablespoon of butter for 2 or 3 minutes, or until they are soft. Add 1 tablespoon of mild prepared mustard (*moutarde de Dijon* if you can get it) dissolved in ½ cup of dry white wine, 1 teaspoon of minced parsley, and salt and pepper. Simmer the sauce 2 more minutes, slice the steak on a hot platter, London-broil fashion, pour the sauce over it and serve immediately.

119

WHEAT FIELDS NEAR CHÂTEAU-THIERRY   *Champagne*

French Bread

Pain de Ménage

(Flour, water, yeast, salt, sugar, butter or egg white)

Making your own French bread is not really as enormous an effort as you may think. To get a crust on the loaves that is as wonderfully tender as it is crisp, be sure to put a large shallow pan of boiling water on the lowest rack of the oven during the baking.

In a large bowl dissolve 1 envelope of dried yeast, 2 teaspoons of salt and 1 tablespoon of sugar in 2 cups of lukewarm water. Mix in gradually 4 or more cups of sifted flour, until the mixture absorbs no more flour. Knead the dough on a floured board until it is slightly elastic, or for about 3 or 4 minutes. Let it rise for 1 hour in a greased bowl, covered with a damp cloth, in a warm corner of the kitchen.

Butter a cookie sheet, sprinkle it with corn meal and shake off the excess. Without working the dough too much, divide it into 2 parts and shape them into long narrow loaves on the cookie sheet. Mark a row of diagonal slits across the tops with a sharp knife and let the loaves rise another 45 minutes. Brush them lightly with melted butter or egg white and bake them in a pre-heated 450° oven for 5 minutes, then lower the temperature to 375° and bake them another 35 minutes.

120

THE ANCIENT COVERED MARKET — DOMME   *Périgord*

Chicken Marengo

Poulet Marengo

(Chicken, garlic, tomatoes, white wine, tomato paste, mushrooms)

Cut a small roasting chicken into serving pieces and salt and pepper them. In a large skillet sauté the pieces in 2 tablespoons of oil and 1 tablespoon of butter until they are brown on all sides and almost cooked through. Remove the chicken and keep it warm. In a small saucepan simmer a dozen mushroom caps in ¾ cup of salted water for 5 minutes, drain them and reserve the water.

To the juices left in the skillet add 1 finely minced clove of garlic and a heaping teaspoon of flour. Blend the mixture well, add 2 large ripe tomatoes, peeled, seeded and chopped, simmer them a few minutes and add ½ cup of dry white wine and ½ cup of the mushroom liquor. Simmer the sauce, uncovered, for 15 minutes and add 1 tablespoon of tomato paste and salt and pepper to taste. Return the chicken to the skillet, add the mushrooms and simmer all together for 5 minutes. Serves four.

FARMHOUSE IN PASSY   *Nivernais*

Jellied Ham with Parsley
Jambon Persillé
(Ham, chicken stock, herbs, shallots, white wine, gelatin, parsley)

This is a family version of a Burgundian specialty which is usually presented, by expert chefs, elaborately molded and made of pieces of a whole ham.

Cut enough leftover ham into small chunks to make 4 cups of lean meat. Simmer 3 cups of chicken stock or consommé with 1 teaspoon of minced fresh tarragon, a *bouquet garni*, 2 chopped shallots, and 1 cup of dry white wine for 20 minutes. Strain the stock through a cheesecloth and stir in 2 envelopes of gelatin, dissolved in ½ cup of cold stock, and 1 tablespoon of tarragon vinegar. Put the ham in a glass serving bowl and pour over it just enough of the stock to half cover it. Put the remaining stock in the refrigerator and when it just begins to thicken stir in 4 tablespoons of finely minced parsley. Pour the stock over the ham and chill the *jambon persillé* thoroughly before serving.

122

THE ANCIENT CHÂTEAU — FOIX   *Comté de Foix*

Cheese Soufflé

Soufflé au Fromage

(Butter, flour, milk, Swiss cheese, Parmesan cheese, eggs)

Make a thick cream sauce with 4 tablespoons of butter, 4 tablespoons of flour, 2 cups of milk, and salt, pepper and a pinch of nutmeg. Simmer the sauce, stirring constantly, for 5 minutes; then stir ¾ cup each of grated Swiss cheese and grated Parmesan into the hot sauce. When the mixture is smooth, take the pan off the fire, let it cool and add slowly 5 beaten egg yolks, stirring constantly.

Beat 6 egg whites stiff but not dry and fold one third of them carefully but thoroughly into the mixture; then fold in the rest very lightly. Pour the batter into 1 large or 2 small buttered soufflé molds. The mold should not be more than ¾ full. Bake the soufflé in a 375° oven for 20 minutes, or until it is puffed high and delicately browned. Serve immediately, of course. Serves six.

THE GOTHIC BRIDGE — ST. AFFRIQUE *Gascony*

Francine's Apple Fritters
Beignets de Pommes à la Francine
(Apples, rum, sugar, and a batter of flour, water, oil, egg)

In a small bowl blend 3 tablespoons of flour smoothly into 4 tablespoons of lukewarm water. Stir in 1 lightly beaten egg yolk mixed with 1½ tablespoons of oil and a pinch of salt. Add a few drops of water if the mixture is too thick and set it aside to rest at room temperature for 2 hours. The batter should just coat the spoon like heavy cream. (It can be used, incidentally, for almost any fruit or vegetable of your choice.)

Shortly before servingtime, peel and core 2 medium apples, slice them into rings ¼ inch thick and sprinkle the slices lightly with rum and sugar. Beat one egg white stiff but not dry, and with a spoon fold it very gently but thorougly into the batter. Heat vegetable oil ½ inch deep in a large frying pan. It will be the right temperature (about 360°) when a 1-inch cube of bread browns in it in 60 seconds. Dip the slices of apple in the batter, coating both sides, drop them in the hot oil and fry them, turning them once, until they are golden brown on both sides. Drain the fritters on brown paper, sprinkle them with sugar and serve them immediately. Serves four.

PALAIS DU LUXEMBOURG   *Paris*

Chestnut Turkey Stuffing
Farce de Dinde aux Marrons

(Chestnuts, shallots, sausage, bread crumbs, celery, mushrooms, brandy, Madeira)

For a 15-pound Thanksgiving turkey prepare the following stuffing: Peel 2 pounds of chestnuts and boil them in salted water until they are tender (or use canned chestnuts packed in brine). In a large skillet sauté 2 shallots and 1 onion, all chopped, in 1 tablespoon of butter. Add ½ pound of sausage meat, heat it briefly, pour off the excess fat and mix in 1½ cups of bread crumbs moistened with ½ cup of hot chicken stock or consommé. Add the chestnuts, crumbled, 2 stalks of celery and 6 mushrooms, all chopped, 1 tablespoon of minced parsley, 1 teaspoon of dried thyme, salt and pepper, ¼ cup of brandy and, if possible, 2 tablespoons of Madeira. (A French chef would use a 2-ounce can of truffles, chopped with their juice, instead of the mushrooms.) Mix the stuffing thoroughly, cool it, and pack it loosely inside the turkey.

TIMBERED SIDE STREET — MOULINS   *Bourbonnais*

Braised Endive
Endives Braisées
(Endive, butter, onion, parsley)

For each serving use 2 plump heads of endive, 1 teaspoon of butter and 3 tablespoons of water. Cook the endive over a very low flame in a tightly covered, heavy saucepan with the butter, water, a few slices of onion, a sprig of parsley and a sprinkling of salt and freshly ground pepper. The liquid should be absorbed and the endive should be cooked through and just beginning to glaze in about 30 minutes. Serve them with a dusting of finely chopped parsley.

THE SHELTERED WALK TO CHENONCEAUX *Touraine*

Fresh Stewed Fruit with Mousseline Sauce

Compote, Sauce Mousseline

(Pears, peaches, cherries, with a sauce of sugar, cream, eggs, sweet wine)

Boil 1 cup of sugar with 1 cup of water for 5 minutes. Add a few drops of vanilla and in this syrup poach 2 firm pears and 2 peaches, all peeled and halved, and a dozen or so ripe black cherries. Remove each piece of fruit when it is tender but still firm and serve the compote hot, with a frothy *sauce mousseline:*

In the top of a double boiler over barely simmering water beat together with a sauce whisk ½ cup of cream, 2 tablespoons of sugar and 3 egg yolks beaten with 2 egg whites. Stir the sauce constantly and when it has thickened, beat in 3 table-spoons of Marsala (or Madeira or sherry). Serves four.

THE CATHEDRAL SQUARE—STRASBOURG *Alsace*

Mirasol Pork and Veal Pâté
Terrine de Viande Mirasol
(Pork, veal, sausage meat, bacon, olive oil, white wine, herbs, spices)

Cut 1 pound each of lean fresh pork and veal into ¼-inch slices and cut the slices into 2-inch squares. Marinate the meat for 24 hours in ½ cup of olive oil and 1 cup of dry white wine, with 1 onion, 2 cloves of garlic and 2 shallots, all chopped, 1 sliced carrot, 2 sprigs of parsley, 2 bay leaves, ½ teaspoon of thyme, salt, pepper and grated nutmeg. Line the bottom and sides of an earthenware *terrine* (an ovenproof dish with a lid) with bacon. Fill the *terrine* with alternating layers of the marinated meat, drained and free of herbs, and fresh sausage meat (about 1 pound). Fill the *terrine* with the strained marinade barely to the level of the top layer of meat, and cover the pâté with more bacon.

Make a stiff paste of flour and water, shape it into a narrow roll and fit the roll around the edge of the *terrine*. Press the lid on firmly and bake the sealed pâté in a 300° oven for 3 hours. Take off the lid and the flour paste, cover the pâté with aluminum foil and cool it under pressure, using any handy object heavy enough to pack the meat down firmly. Chill the pâté for 2 days before serving it sliced, as an hors-d'oeuvre or with salad.

128

THE CLASSIC FOUNTAIN—ARBOIS   *Franche-Comté*

Eggs in Aspic with Madeira

Oeufs en Gelée au Madère

(Eggs, consommé, gelatin, Madeira, tarragon, ham)

Boil 6 eggs for 6 minutes, cool them under running water and shell them carefully when they are cold. Soak 1 tablespoon of gelatin in ¼ cup of cold water. Heat 1½ cups of clear chicken consommé, add the gelatin and stir until it dissolves completely. Add 2 tablespoons of Madeira (or port or sherry) and set this aspic aside to cool.

Use small molds or ramekins just wide and deep enough to hold 1 egg each with a little space to spare. Trim 6 thin slices of ham just to fit the tops of the molds. Spoon a little aspic into the bottom of each mold to make a layer about ¼ inch thick. When this is almost firm, decorate it with 2 crossed leaves of fresh tarragon or a tiny sprig of parsley. Gently place an egg in each ramekin, spoon aspic over them until the molds are almost full, and cover each egg with a circle of ham. Glaze the ham with a final spoonful of aspic, chill the eggs and serve them unmolded.

129

VILLAGE ON THE LOIRE — ST. MATHURIN *Anjou*

Black Pepper Steak
Steak au Poivre
(Steak, peppercorns, butter, white wine)

Use a good cut of beef, trimmed and cut at least 1½ inches thick, about 2 pounds for 4 people. Cover both sides of the steak very generously with peppercorns first coarsely crushed in a mortar or on a board with a potato masher. Pound the pepper firmly into the meat with the potato masher. In an iron skillet, over a high flame, brown both sides of the steak in 1 tablespoon of butter and a few drops of oil. A French cook would, of course, leave the steak rare. When it is done, remove it to a hot platter. Stir ½ cup dry white wine (and 1 table-spoon of brandy, if you wish) into the pan juices, simmer the sauce for 2 minutes, add a lump of butter and pour it, loose pepper and all, over the steak. Serve with French-fried potatoes.

CHÂTEAU D'O, NEAR MORTRÉE   *Normandy*

Flambéed Apricot Omelette

Omelette Flambée aux Abricots

(Eggs, apricot preserves, almonds, rum, whipped cream)

Make a 6-egg omelette and when it is cooked through but still soft spread across the center ⅓ cup of apricot preserves and a few slivers of blanched almonds. Fold the omelette and turn it out on a platter. Sprinkle the top with sugar and a few more almonds and pour on 3 tablespoons of warmed rum. Light the rum, bring the omelette flaming to the table and serve it with a bowl of chilled whipped cream flavored with sugar and almond extract. Serves four.

THE CITY HALL—BORDEAUX

Bordelais

Roast Beef Bordeaux
Rôti de Boeuf à la Bordelaise

(Rump roast of beef, white wine, olive oil, onion, shallots, herbs, vinegar)

Remove the fat from a 3-pound rump roast of beef and reserve it. Marinate the meat overnight in 1 cup of white wine and ½ cup of olive oil, with 1 sliced onion, 2 chopped shallots, 1 bay leaf, several sprigs of parsley, ¼ teaspoon of thyme, and salt and pepper.

Spread part of the beef fat in the bottom of the roasting pan, add the chopped vegetables from the marinade, and put in the roast, lightly salted and with a strip of beef fat tied over the top with kitchen string. Pour in ¼ cup of the marinade and roast the meat, uncovered, in a 350° oven for 1¼ hours, basting it often. Remove the roast to a hot platter and cut off the string. Strain the pan juices into a saucepan, add the rest of the marinade, and simmer the sauce over a good flame to reduce it a little. Let it stand for a few minutes until the excess fat rises to the top, skim off the fat, and add a dash of wine vinegar. Reheat and serve in a sauceboat.

CHÂTEAU DE LOCHES *Touraine*

Cheese Tart

Tarte au Fromage Touraine

(Pastry, Swiss cheese, eggs, cream, spices)

Line a 9-inch pie pan with a thin layer of rich pastry dough and chill it. Beat 4 eggs thoroughly and combine them with 1½ cups of cream and ½ pound of grated Swiss cheese. Season with grated nutmeg, a touch of cayenne pepper, and salt to taste. Pour this filling into the pie shell, bake the *tarte* in a preheated 400° oven for 15 minutes, then lower the heat to 325°. The cheese custard should be set and golden brown in about 30 minutes. Serve directly from the pan.

MARKET DAY IN PONT L'ABBÉ *Brittany*

Fish Salad with Ravigote Sauce

Salade de Poisson Ravigote

(Fish fillets, eggs, anchovies and a sauce of mayonnaise, herbs, seasonings)

Simmer together for 20 minutes 2 cups each of white wine and water with 1 teaspoon of salt, 1 small carrot and 1 small onion, both sliced, a few peppercorns and a *bouquet garni*. In this *court-bouillon* poach 1½ pounds of white fish (bass, pike or Lake Michigan whitefish would be good choices) until it is cooked but still whole and firm. Drain the fish and chill it.

Fillet the fish, cut it into serving pieces and arrange each one on a green lettuce leaf on a serving platter. Split 4 hard-boiled eggs lengthwise, place an anchovy fillet on each one and arrange these between the pieces of fish. Mask each fish fillet with a generous spoonful of *sauce ravigote:*

To ¾ cup of mayonnaise add 1 teaspoon of lemon juice, 2 tablespoons of cream, 1 shallot and 2 small sour gherkins, all finely chopped, 2 teaspoons each of capers and minced parsley, 1 teaspoon of chopped chives and a little freshly ground pepper. Let the sauce steep for an hour or two before using it. Serves four.

THE RIVERBANK — BAYONNE   *Béarn*

Ham Mousse

Mousse au Jambon

(Ham, chicken stock, gelatin, eggs, cream, Port)

Put enough cooked ham through the finest blade of a meat grinder to make
3½ cups. Grind the ham several times if necessary, to give it a very fine, smooth
consistency. Dissolve 1 envelope of gelatin in ¼ cup of chicken stock. Heat
another 1¼ cup of stock in a saucepan and stir the gelatin mixture into it. Beat
2 egg yolks lightly in a bowl and gradually stir in the warm chicken stock. Return
this mixture to the saucepan, reheat it, stirring constantly, until it just begins to
thicken, then set it aside to cool.

Whip ½ cup of cream and beat 2 egg whites stiff. Mix together the ground
ham, the thickened chicken stock and the whipped cream. Stir in 4 tablespoons
of Port and then fold in the beaten egg whites. Pour the mousse into a mold
and chill it for at least 3 hours. Turn it out onto a platter and garnish it with
water cress and unpeeled, thinly sliced cucumber just before serving.

TOWN HALL—MOLSHEIM   *Alsace*

Roast Leg of Veal with Mustard

Rôti de Veau à la Moutarde

(Veal roast, butter, mustard, stock)

Salt and pepper a roast of veal and place it in an open roasting pan. Cream together equal amounts of butter and mild prepared mustard, preferably *moutarde de Dijon,* and spread half of this generously on the meat. Roast the veal in a 300° oven for 30 minutes per pound for a leg, breast or shoulder, 40 minutes per pound for a loin or rolled roast, basting often with the pan juices, and adding a little chicken stock if the pan gets dry. When the roast is half done, spread it with the rest of the mustard and butter mixture. When the meat is done, remove it to a hot platter. Dilute the pan juices with a little hot chicken stock and serve them in a sauceboat. Serve with buttered noodles.

PATHWAY BY THE SEINE—PETIT ANDELY   *Normandy*

Normandy Roast Duck Champsaur

Caneton Champsaur

(Duck, russet apples, bread, cinnamon, white wine, stock, Calvados, cream)

Sauté 1 cup of diced soft white bread in 2 tablespoons of hot butter until it is lightly browned. Peel, core and chop coarsely enough tart or russet apples to make 2 cups and add them to the bread. Cook until the apples begin to soften. Season this stuffing with ⅛ teaspoon of cinnamon, and salt and freshly ground pepper. Moisten it with a very little white wine.

Stuff the duck, truss it, and rub it with salt and pepper. Roast it, uncovered, in a 325° oven for 20 to 25 minutes per pound; prick the skin several times to release the fat. Add ½ cup each of white wine and chicken stock (or consommé) to the roasting pan and baste the duck often. When the duck is done, remove it to a hot platter and skim most of the fat from the pan juices. Pour in 2 tablespoons of Calvados or apple brandy and ¼ cup of heavy cream. Reheat the sauce, stirring briskly, and pour it through a strainer into a sauceboat.

F   137

THE WOODED HILLS, NEAR ST. NECTAIRE   *Auvergne*

Pork Chop Casserole
Côtes de Porc à l'Auvergnate

(Pork chops, cabbage, cream, white wine, sage, grated cheese)

Remove the outside leaves of a small young cabbage, slice it finely and boil it for 7 minutes in salted water. Drain the cabbage thoroughly, add salt and pepper and 1 cup of cream, and simmer it, covered, for 30 minutes. Meanwhile, in an iron skillet sauté 4 lean, well-trimmed pork chops in a little butter until they are brown and cooked through. Remove the chops and season them with salt and freshly ground pepper. Stir ½ cup of white wine briskly into the pan juices, add a good pinch of sage and simmer the mixture for a couple of minutes. Stir this juice into the creamed cabbage.

Spread half of the cabbage in the bottom of an ovenproof casserole. Add the pork chops, cover them with the rest of the cabbage, sprinkle generously with grated Parmesan and a little melted butter, and bake the casserole, uncovered, in a 350° oven for 20 minutes, or until the top is golden brown. Serves four.

THE ARCHED CLIFF — ÉTRETAT *Normandy*

Fresh Shrimp Pâté

Pâté de Crevettes

(Shrimp, lemon, seasoning, olive oil)

Shell and devein ½ pound of cooked shrimp and put them twice through the finest blade of a meat grinder. Add 3 tablespoons of lemon juice, freshly ground pepper, a generous dash of paprika and a pinch of salt, and mix well. Then add gradually about ½ cup of olive oil, blending the shrimp to a creamy paste. Store the pâté in a covered jar in the refrigerator and serve it on circles of toast or crackers.

139

RESTAURANT LAPÉROUSE *Paris*

Cold Madrilène Consommé
Consommé Madrilène
(Chicken stock or consommé, tomatoes, celery salt, herbs)

This is one of the simpler ways to make one of the great soups of classic cuisine. You can use canned chicken consommé, or make your own chicken stock by boiling the carcass and bones of a roast chicken with the neck and giblets, 1 carrot and 1 onion, both cut in pieces, 1 stalk of celery, several peppercorns, salt, a *bouquet garni* and enough water to cover well. Simmer the stock until it is reduced and flavorful. For each cup of strained stock add 1 small ripe tomato, peeled, seeded and chopped, and celery salt and freshly ground pepper to taste. Simmer the madrilène for 30 minutes, strain it through a fine sieve or cheesecloth and serve it chilled with a little minced parsley and chives.

THE GOTHIC PORTAL — CHÂTEAU DE BLOIS *Orléanais*

Honey Cakes

Gâteaux au Miel

(Eggs, sugar, honey, flour)

Blend thoroughly ½ cup of sugar and a scant ¼ cup of honey into 2 well-beaten eggs. Sift 1 cup of flour and mix it gradually into the batter which should remain quite thin. Set it aside to rest for 45 minutes, then spread it about ⅜ inch thick on a buttered cookie sheet and bake the *gâteau* in a 375° oven for 20 minutes. Cut it in squares while it is still hot and transfer the squares to a cake rack to cool and harden.

ANGRY SEAS AT PARAMÉ *Brittany*

Baked Turbot (or Halibut) in Cream

Turbot au Four à la Crème

(Turbot, mushrooms, onions, bay leaf, garlic, white wine, cream, new potatoes)

Wipe a 3-pound piece of turbot or halibut with a cloth and rub it with a little flour seasoned with salt and pepper. Put the fish in a generously buttered baking dish and dot it with 4 tablespoons of butter. Bake the fish in a 350° oven for 20 minutes and baste it often. Then add ½ pound of whole button mushrooms, ¾ cup of thinly sliced white onions, 1 bay leaf, 1 cut clove of garlic and 1 cup of dry white wine. Cover the baking dish with a piece of buttered brown paper to keep the fish from drying and bake it for another 20 minutes, still basting it frequently. Transfer the fish, mushrooms and onions to a heated platter and discard the bay leaf and garlic. To the liquid left in the baking dish add 1 cup of warm heavy cream. Heat the sauce to the boiling point, taste it for seasoning and pour it over the fish. Finish the platter with boiled new potatoes and several decorative sprigs of parsley. Serves six.

THE STATELY METROPOLIS — BORDEAUX *Bordelais*

Broiled Lamb Kidneys

Rognons de Mouton en Brochette

(Lamb kidneys, water cress, butter, parsley, broiled tomatoes)

For each serving soak 2 lamb kidneys in cold water for 20 minutes. Remove the skin and split the kidneys from the rounded sides, leaving the two halves attached on the indented side. Run a skewer into the cut surface of one half and then back through the other half from the outside, so as to hold the kidney flat on the skewer. Season the kidneys with salt and pepper, brush them with oil and grill them under a hot broiler for 3 minutes on each side. Serve the *brochettes* on a bed of water cress and on each kidney put a small lump of butter creamed with minced parsley. Garnish the platter with broiled tomatoes.

THE RHÔNE VALLEY AT BEAUCAIRE   *Provence*

Chicken Casserole from Southern France
Poule en Cocotte du Midi
(Fowl, onions, bacon, herbs, tomatoes, carrots, red wine, brandy)

Cut a fowl into serving pieces and salt and pepper them. Heat 3 tablespoons of salad oil in an iron *cocotte* or a heavy casserole and add 4 small whole onions (or a large one, quartered), 3 slices of bacon, diced, and a *bouquet garni*. Add the pieces of chicken and brown them on all sides. Add 4 peeled and seeded tomatoes, 2 carrots, cut in pieces, 2 cups of red wine and a liqueur glass of brandy. Cover the casserole and let the chicken simmer over a low fire for about 2½ hours, or until it is very tender. Add more wine or a little chicken consommé during the cooking if the sauce reduces too quickly. Serves four to six.

144

RESTAURANT "MAISON DES TÊTES"—COLMAR   *Alsace*

Ham with Madeira Sauce

Jambon, Sauce Madère

(Baked ham, onion, flour, tomato paste, chicken consommé, Madeira, spinach)

In a heavy saucepan sauté 1 small minced onion in 1 teaspoon of butter until it is soft. Blend in 1 teaspoon of flour and brown it lightly, stirring briskly. Stir in 1 teaspoon of tomato paste, add 1½ cups of chicken consommé, and simmer the sauce over a low flame until it is reduced to about 1 cup. Just before servingtime, heat but do not brown 8 thin slices of baked ham in a skillet with a little butter. Spread a bed of well-drained purée of spinach on a hot platter and arrange the ham on top. Add 2 tablespoons of Madeira to the hot sauce, strain it over the ham, and serve immediately. Serves four.

F   145

CHÂTEAU DE SAUMUR *Anjou*

Eggplant Purée

Purée d'Aubergines

(Eggplant, shallots, chicken consommé, milk, nutmeg, butter)

Peel 2 medium eggplants and cut them into ¾-inch dice. Put them in a heavy saucepan with 3 minced shallots, ⅓ cup of chicken stock or consommé, 2 table-spoons of milk, and salt, freshly ground pepper and a pinch of nutmeg. Cook the eggplant, covered, over low heat for about 25 minutes, or until it is quite soft. Force it through a strainer; if the purée is too thin, reduce it quickly over high heat. Add a good lump of butter and sprinkle with chopped parsley before serving. Serves four.

146

REFLECTION IN THE YONNE—JOIGNY   *Burgundy*

Burgundian Snails

Escargots de Bourgogne

(Canned snails, butter, parsley, garlic, nutmeg)

Providing one is equipped with a taste for garlic and a set of metal snail dishes, shell-shaped clamps and little two-pronged forks, this famous specialty should present no serious problems even to the amateur cook. The classic Burgundian butter sauce is simplicity itself. The snails are imported in quantity nowadays, with the snails in a can and their shells usually in a separate package; the shells are reuseable.

Allow 6 snails per person for a first course, or a full dozen for a main course. They can be prepared well in advance, chilled, and heated at the last moment. For four dozen snails, cream together 1¾ sticks of butter, ½ cup of minced parsley, 8 to 10 minced and crushed cloves of garlic, 4 or 5 minced shallots, a pinch of nutmeg, and pepper and just a little salt to taste. Wash and drain the shells. Drain the brine from the canned snails, place one in each shell, and pack the shells brim-full with the garlic butter. Arrange them carefully, open ends up, in the hollows of the snail dishes, and heat them in a 450° oven until they are bubbling hot. Serve them in the same dishes, with plenty of French bread for mopping up the melted butter.

147

LAC DE NANTUA   *Bresse*

Shrimp Nantua

Crevettes Sautées Nantua

(Shrimp, mushrooms, tomato paste, cream)

This is an adaptation of an elaborate provincial specialty which is usually made with fresh-water crayfish.

Boil 2 pounds of shrimp for 5 minutes, cool them and shell them. Over a very low flame simmer the shrimp in 4 tablespoons of butter for about 10 minutes, turning each one at least once. Add ½ pound of sliced mushrooms and simmer them another 5 minutes. Sprinkle the mixture with 2 teaspoons of flour and blend it in thoroughly. Dilute 1½ teaspoons of tomato paste with a little heavy cream, add enough cream to make 1¾ cups in all and pour it over the shrimp. Season the sauce with salt and freshly ground white pepper and simmer it gently for a few minutes until it thickens somewhat. Serve *crevettes Nantua* in individual ramekins or scallop shells. Serves six to eight.

THE CATHEDRAL OF ST. ETIENNE—AUXERRE *Burgundy*

Veal Birds à la Française

Paupiettes de Veau

(Veal scallops, sausage meat, bread crumbs, milk, eggs, parsley, white wine, cream)

On a chopping board pound 8 veal scallops quite thin with a wooden potato masher. Trim them to even rectangles and add the scraps, finely minced, to the following stuffing: Mix together ¼ pound of sausage meat, ½ cup of crumbled stale bread soaked in hot milk and squeezed dry, 1 beaten egg, 1 tablespoon of minced parsley, and a little black pepper. Spread the stuffing on the scallops, roll them up and tie them neatly with kitchen thread. Melt 2 tablespoons of butter in a skillet, add the veal birds and simmer them, without browning too much and turning several times, for ½ hour. Then add ½ cup of white wine or stock and braise the *paupiettes* slowly for 1 hour, or until they are glazed brown and tender. Transfer them to a heated platter and cut off the threads. Deglaze the skillet with a little hot stock and ¼ cup of thin cream, and stir this sauce briskly over a good flame for 2 or 3 minutes. Pour the sauce over the *paupiettes* and serve immediately with sautéed mushroom caps. Serves four.

149

SIDE PORTAL OF THE CATHEDRAL—METZ   *Lorraine*

Baked Eggs Lorraine

Oeufs sur le Plat Lorraine

(Eggs, ham, Swiss gruyère, cream)

Butter individual shirred-egg dishes. In each one put first a thin slice of ham, then a thin slice of Swiss gruyère. Break 2 eggs into each dish and pour over them 2 tablespoons of heavy cream. Sprinkle sparingly with salt and pepper. Bake the *oeufs Lorraine* in a 350° oven for 10 minutes, or until the cheese has melted, the whites are set, but the yolks are still soft.

THE FLEET AT ST. VALERY-SUR-SOMME   *Picardy*

Lobster Bisque

Bisque de Homard

(Lobster, chicken consommé, white wine, seasonings, cream, egg yolks, sherry)

In a soup kettle heat together 4 cups of chicken stock or consommé, 2 cups of water and 1 cup of dry white wine, with 1 stalk of celery and 1 onion, both cut in pieces, 4 crushed peppercorns, 1 bay leaf, a pinch of thyme and a sprig of parsley. When this *court-bouillon* has simmered for 15 minutes, boil a live 2-pound lobster in it for 20 minutes. Remove the lobster and strain the stock through a fine sieve. Let the lobster cool, remove the meat and set it aside. Discard the large claw shells, and break the rest of the carcass and shell into pieces and reserve it.

Heat 4 cups of the stock in the top of a large double boiler, stir in 2 tablespoons of butter creamed with 3 tablespoons of flour, and add 1 cup of thin cream. Add the reserved shells and cook the bisque over simmering water for 1 hour, stirring occasionally. Shortly before servingtime, strain the bisque again, return it to the double boiler, and add ¼ cup of sherry and ½ cup of heavy cream mixed with 3 lightly beaten egg yolks. Taste the bisque for seasoning, reheat it, stirring until it thickens a little, and garnish it with pieces of claw meat. (See Lobster Canapés in the *Index* for one way to use up the rest of the meat.) Serves six.

151

CHÂTEAU DE PUYGILHEM   *Périgord*

Veal Steak Gratiné

Rouelle de Veau au Gratin

(Veal steak, bacon, shallots, parsley, bread crumbs, chicken consommé)

Use a thick veal steak cut from the leg, weighing about 1½ pounds. Put the steak in a shallow well-buttered baking dish and cover it with a mixture of 3 tablespoons of finely chopped bacon, 2 chopped shallots, 2 tablespoons of chopped parsley, pepper and a little salt, and sprinkle these seasonings with fine bread crumbs. Add ½ cup of chicken consommé and bake the steak in a 300° oven for 1¼ hours, or until it is tender and well browned. Baste it occasionally with the juices in the dish, adding a little consommé if necessary. Serve from the baking dish, garnished with parsley and slices of lemon. Serves four.

HILLSIDE FARM LANDS   *Guyenne*

Veal Chops with Mushrooms and Cream
Côtes de Veau à la Crème

(Veal chops, butter, button mushrooms, cream, egg yolks, sherry)

In a heavy skillet, over high heat, brown 4 thick loin veal chops well on both sides in 2 tablespoons of hot butter. When they are brown, lower the heat, cover the skillet, and simmer them for 20 to 25 minutes, turning them once and adding butter sparingly if they tend to stick. Five minutes before the chops are done, drain a 2-ounce can of button mushrooms, reserving the juice, and add the mushrooms to the skillet. Then remove the chops to a hot platter and keep them warm. Pour the juice from the mushrooms into the skillet and stir well, scrapping up all the brown scraps. Add ¾ cup of cream mixed with 2 egg yolks and 1 tablespoon of sherry or Madeira, season to taste with salt and pepper, and heat the sauce slowly without letting it boil, stirring constantly, until it thickens. Pour the sauce and mushrooms over the chops and serve them with noodles or rice.

BASQUE VILLAGE—AÏNHOA *Béarn*

Basque Rice

Riz à la Basquaise

(Rice, butter, chicken stock, onions, sweet pepper, olive oil)

Heat 1 cup of raw rice in 2 tablespoons of melted butter, stirring often, until every grain is coated and it begins to turn golden. Add 1 cup of chicken stock or consommé and bring it to a boil, then lower the flame and cook the rice, covered, for 15 minutes, or until all the liquid has been absorbed. Add another 2½ cups of hot chicken stock and continue cooking the rice very slowly, still covered, until all the liquid has been absorbed. Meanwhile, in a skillet, sauté 3 medium onions, chopped, and 1 sweet red or green pepper, diced, in 3 tablespoons of butter or olive oil until they are cooked through and golden. Mix the vegetables and rice together with a fork and add a little freshly ground pepper. Serves four.

154

LA MALLERIE, NEAR PLOUBALAY   *Brittany*

Caramel Baked Pears

Poires Joséphine

(Anjou pears, sugar, butter, cream)

Arrange 6 firm Anjou pears, peeled, quartered and cored, in one closely packed layer in a shallow baking dish. Sprinkle them generously with granulated sugar and dot them with 4 tablespoons of butter cut in small bits. Put them in the hottest possible preheated oven and bake them until the sugar is brown and caramelized. Then add ¾ to 1 cup of heavy cream, spoon the caramelized juice and the cream over the pears to blend the sauce, and serve them warm, from the baking dish. Serves four to six.

DEAD-END STREET—POUILLY-SUR-LOIRE *Nivernais*

Celery Root with Rémoulade Sauce
Céleri Rémoulade

(Celery root, with a sauce of egg yolks, mustard, vinegar, olive oil, herbs)

This classic of the French hors-d'oeuvre tray is very little trouble if you have a good vegetable shredder. Choose celery roots (celeriac) that are not too large and pare off all the fibrous outside. Cut the roots into chunks and put them through the shredder, using a blade that cuts strips about ⅛ inch wide.

For 2 cups of shredded celery root, mash together 1 hard-boiled and 1 raw egg yolk. Add 1½ teaspoons of strong Dijon mustard (or 1 tablespoon of mild American mustard), salt, pepper, and 2 tablespoons of tarragon vinegar. Work the mixture to a smooth paste and add bit by bit ½ cup of cold olive oil, stirring constantly until the sauce thickens like mayonnaise. Mix the dressing and celery root together, chill, and sprinkle with minced parsley and chives before serving.

MARKET DAY IN TULLE   *Limousin*

Sardine-stuffed Tomatoes

Tomates Galloise

(Tomatoes, sardines, hard-boiled eggs, water cress, seasonings)

Cut off the stem ends of tomatoes, remove the center core and the seeds, and let the tomatoes drain, cut side down, for an hour or two. The proportions for the stuffing are about 3 medium sardines to 1 hard-boiled egg to ¼ cup of chopped water cress. Drain the sardines, take off the skin if it is coarse, and mash them with a fork. Chop the whites of the eggs and mash the yolks. Mix sardines, eggs and water cress together and season the mixture well with lemon juice, chives, capers, mustard, pepper, and a little salt and olive oil. Stuff the tomatoes and garnish the tops with a slice of hard-boiled egg and 3 or 4 whole water cress leaves. Serve as an hors-d'oeuvre, with French bread and sweet butter.

157

ROMANESQUE PORCH—ST. GILLES   *Languedoc*

Squab with New Peas

Pigeons aux Petits Pois

(Squab, bacon, onions, chicken consommé, green peas, lettuce, bouquet garni)

Squab or Rock Cornish game birds may be used. For 6 tiny birds or 3 larger ones, in a casserole brown lightly 2 strips of diced bacon in 2 tablespoons of hot butter. Remove the bacon and reserve it, and brown 8 to 10 tiny whole onions, or 3 or 4 medium ones, quartered, in the casserole. Remove the onions and reserve them, and in the remaining fat brown the birds evenly on all sides. Take them out, and if there is too much fat in the casserole, pour off all but 2 tablespoons. Blend ½ tablespoon of flour into the remaining fat and when the *roux* is golden brown, add gradually ½ cup of chicken consommé. Bring the mixture to a boil once, stirring constantly, then return the birds, the bacon and the onions to the casserole and add a *bouquet garni*. Cover the casserole and bake it in a 400° oven for 45 minutes to 1 hour, depending on the size of the birds. Thirty minutes before the cooking time is up, add 3 cups of young green peas and 2 or 3 lettuce leaves. To serve, discard the *bouquet garni* and arrange the birds on a deep platter with the vegetables and sauce around them. Serves six.

PLACE DES VOSGES   *Paris*

Beef Tenderloin with Mushroom Sauce

Filet aux Champignons

(Beef tenderloin, mushrooms, butter, sherry, brandy, cream, mustard)

Sauté ½ pound of sliced fresh mushrooms in 2 tablespoons of butter for 5 minutes or until they are soft. Add salt and pepper and 2 tablespoons of dry sherry. Put a match to 1 tablespoon of warmed brandy and pour it flaming over the mushrooms. Shake the pan until the flame dies out, then add 3 tablespoons of cream blended with 1 teaspoon of flour and 1 tablespoon of mild Dijon mustard. Simmer all together, stirring often, until the sauce is slightly reduced.

Meanwhile, in a skillet over a moderate flame, brown 4 1-inch-thick slices of tenderloin of beef in a little hot butter for 2½ minutes on each side. They should be well browned, but rare inside. Transfer them to a hot platter and pour the mushroom sauce over them. Serves four.

ROMAN ARCH—ST. RÉMY   *Provence*

Artichokes Barigoule
Artichauts Barigoule

(Artichokes, mushrooms, onion, garlic, ham, herbs, white wine, stock, olive oil)

Trim the bases of 4 artichokes and cut ½ inch from the tips of the leaves. Parboil them in salted water for 20 minutes, drain them, and remove the thin center leaves and the chokes. Meanwhile, sauté lightly ¼ pound of mushrooms, 1 small onion and 1 small clove of garlic, all minced, in 2 teaspoons of butter and 1 tablespoon of olive oil. When the vegetables are soft, add ¼ cup each of minced ham and fine bread crumbs, 1 tablespoon of stock, 1 teaspoon of minced parsley, and a little pepper. Mix well and fill the centers of the artichokes with this stuffing. Put 3 tablespoons of olive oil in a small casserole, add the artichokes, 1 small sliced carrot, ½ cup each of dry white wine and chicken stock or consommé, and a *bouquet garni*. Pour a few drops of oil into each artichoke and bring the liquid to a boil on top of the stove. Then bake them, covered, in a 300° oven for 40 minutes, basting occasionally. Serve the artichokes with the juice poured over them. Serves four.

160

TOUR DE L'HORLOGE—AUXERRE   *Burgundy*

Duck with Glazed Onions

Canard aux Oignons Brulés

(Duck, onions, butter, sugar, chicken consommé)

Rub a duck with a little salt and pepper and roast it in a 325° oven for 20 to 25 minutes per pound; prick the skin to release the fat and baste the bird with the pan juices diluted with a spoonful of chicken consommé. Serve it surrounded with a dozen or more onions cooked as follows: In a heavy saucepan sauté whole medium onions gently for 5 minutes in 2 or 3 tablespoons of hot butter, shaking the pan and turning them often. Sprinkle them with 1½ to 2 tablespoons of granulated sugar and cook them another 5 minutes, still turning them often, until they are brown and begin to glaze. Add 1 cup of chicken consommé, and simmer the onions, covered, for 40 minutes, or until they are soft but still whole.

DELACROIX'S STUDIO, PLACE FURSTENBERG   *Paris*

Flambéed Fresh Figs

Figues Flambées Boulestin

(Figs, Curaçao, brandy, heavy cream)

Peel carefully 12 ripe purple figs, leave them whole, and put them in a chafing dish with 3 tablespoons each of Curaçao and brandy. Light the alcohol lamp and in a few seconds put a match to the liqueurs. Prick each fig with a silver fork and shake the pan gently until the flame dies. The figs will be warm and a little softened and the liqueur reduced. Serve immediately and pass a pitcher of heavy cream separately. Serves six.

THE MOUNTAIN TOWN OF GRASSE *Riviera*

Scrambled Eggs Paul Reboux
Oeufs Brouillés Paul Reboux

(Eggs, orange rind, cream, sherry, butter)

Beat 4 eggs lightly with a fork and add the grated rind of half an orange, salt, pepper, and 1 tablespoon each of heavy cream and sherry. Melt a generous lump of butter in a skillet, add the eggs and cook them slowly, stirring constantly with a wire whisk, not a fork, until they achieve a rich creamy consistency. Serve the eggs on hot buttered toast with just a soupçon of grated orange rind on top.

THE GOOD SHIP "BELLE FRANCE"—NICE *Riviera*

Mixed Salad Niçoise with Ravigote Sauce

Macédoine Niçoise, Sauce Ravigote

(Chicken, ham, cheese, herring, eggs, vegetables, French dressing, herbs)

In a wooden salad bowl that has been rubbed with a cut clove of garlic, mix together the following, all cut in thin julienne strips: Enough cold chicken to make about 1 cup; 2 good slices of ham; enough Italian *mortadella* or salami to make ½ cup; 3 herring fillets preserved in oil; the whites of 2 hard-boiled eggs, and 1 medium-sized boiled beet. Then add the following, all diced: 2 cold boiled potatoes, ½ a tart apple, 2 stalks of celery, and 1 green pepper. Finally add the heart of 1 head of lettuce, shredded, and a dozen or more small black Italian or Greek olives.

Just before serving the *macédoine*, pour over it about ¾ cup of *sauce ravigote* —a highly seasoned French dressing made of 1 part wine vinegar, 3 parts olive oil, and salt, pepper, dry mustard, onion and parsley (both minced), orégano, and capers, all added to taste. Mix the salad thoroughly and sprinkle it with the sieved yolks of 2 hard-boiled eggs. Serves four as a salad or eight as an hors-d'oeuvre.

164

RIVERSIDE ARCHITECTURE IN AURILLAC *Auvergne*

French Boiled Dinner

Pot-au-Feu

(Beef, veal knuckle, carrots, turnips, leeks, onion, herbs, cabbage, potatoes)

In a soup kettle put a 4-pound piece of rump of beef, free of fat, a piece of cracked veal knuckle, a piece of beef shin bone, 5 quarts of water, a few whole peppercorns, and 2 tablespoons of salt. Simmer the meat for 2 hours and skim the surface of the bouillon several times. Then add 4 carrots, 2 medium white turnips and 6 small leeks, all cut in pieces, 1 large onion stuck with 3 whole cloves, 1 bay leaf, ½ teaspoon of dried thyme and several sprigs of parsley. Simmer the *pot-au-feu* over a low fire for another 1½ hours. One half hour before servingtime, ladle out enough bouillon to cook separately a small head of cabbage, cut in serving pieces. Traditionally, the strained *pot-au-feu* bouillon, with the fat skimmed off, is served first as a soup course. Then the beef is served sliced, with the vegetables, boiled potatoes, coarse salt and a pot of French mustard. Serves six to eight.

165

CHURCH SPIRE AT BRÉZOLLES   *Orléanais*

Grand Marnier Soufflé

Soufflé Grand Marnier Ile-de-France

(Eggs, sugar, Grand Marnier, cream of tartar, butter)

Separate 10 eggs and put 2 of the yolks aside. In the top of a double boiler beat the 8 remaining yolks until they are lemon colored, then beat in gradually ⅔ cup of granulated sugar. Cook the mixture over barely simmering water, stirring constantly with a whisk. As soon as the yolks have thickened, place the top of the double boiler in a bowl of cracked ice and stir in ½ cup of Grand Marnier. Beat the 10 egg whites with a tiny pinch of cream of tartar until they stand in peaks but are not dry. Transfer the yolk mixture to a bowl and with a rubber spatula fold in thoroughly one third of the whites, then fold in the rest very lightly. Pour the batter into a 2-quart soufflé mold first buttered and sprinkled lightly with sugar. Tie a strip of waxed paper around the mold so that it makes a collar standing about 2 inches above the rim of the mold, and butter the inside of the collar. Bake the soufflé in a preheated 450° oven for 15 minutes. Sprinkle the top lightly with sugar, remove the paper collar, and serve immediately. Serves six.

CONVERSATION—LE PUY   *Auvergne*

White Wine Rabbit Stew

Lapin en Gibelotte

(Rabbit, bacon fat, stock, white wine, garlic, herbs, tomato paste, sour cream)

Have the butcher cut a 4- to 5-pound rabbit into serving pieces. In a casserole brown the pieces on all sides in 3 tablespoons of bacon fat. Sprinkle them with 2 tablespoons of flour, blend well, and add 2 cups each of stock and white wine. Add 1 clove of garlic, chopped, a *bouquet garni*, 2 heaping tablespoons of tomato paste, and salt and pepper. Simmer the rabbit, covered, over low heat for 1½ hours, or until it is tender. Transfer the meat to a platter; reduce the sauce if necessary, stir in 2 tablespoons of sour cream, and strain it over the rabbit. Serves six.

PYRENEES LANDSCAPE *Gascony*

Beef in Onion Sauce
Miroton de Boeuf
(Boiled beef, onions, vinegar, stock, garlic, tomato paste, bread crumbs, Parmesan)

This sturdy dish is intended for leftover boiled beef (see French Boiled Dinner in the *Index*) and is also good for serving leftover roasts hot instead of cold.

In a covered iron skillet simmer 3 large onions, finely chopped, in 3 tablespoons of butter, stirring often. When they are cooked through and golden, but not brown, sprinkle on 1 tablespoon of flour, blend it in thoroughly, and add 2 tablespoons of vinegar, 1 cup of beef stock or consommé, and 2 tablespoons of tomato paste. Season the sauce well with salt, freshly ground pepper and a touch of minced garlic, and simmer it for 20 minutes. Pour half the sauce into a shallow baking dish. On it arrange 8 slices of boiled beef, not too thick, cover them with the rest of the sauce, and sprinkle the dish lightly with bread crumbs and grated Parmesan. Put the *miroton* in a moderate oven until the bread crumbs brown. Serve very hot, with small sour pickles. Serves four.

168

MANOIR DE CAUDEMONE *Normandy*

Fruit Cup with Sherbet and Champagne
Coupe Jacques
(Pineapple, bananas, strawberries, oranges, grapes, kirsch, sherbet, champagne)

Half fill stemmed sherbet glasses with a *macédoine de fruits* made of diced fresh pineapple, bananas, strawberries, oranges, and seedless grapes which have all been marinated and chilled together with a little sugar and kirsch. On the fruit place a scoop of fruit sherbet, preferably lemon, and decorate it with a tiny sprig of mint. At the table open a bottle of chilled dry champagne and pour a little over each *coupe*. Needless to say, one drinks the rest of the champagne, and probably more, with *coupe Jacques*.

MARSEILLES WATER FRONT   *Provence*

Bouillabaisse

Bouillabaisse de Marseille

(Fresh fish and shellfish, olive oil, onion, garlic, tomatoes, herbs, saffron, white wine)

In a soup kettle sauté 1 large onion and 4 cloves of garlic, all minced, in ¾ cup of olive oil until they are golden. Add 2 large ripe tomatoes, peeled, seeded and chopped, 3 tablespoons of chopped parsley, 1 bay leaf, a pinch of thyme, a piece of fennel, 1 teaspoon of dried saffron, and plenty of freshly-ground black pepper. Simmer the mixture for a few minutes and add 2 small lobsters and 3 pounds of fish. Perfection can be achieved only with Mediterranean fish, but a selection of whiting, bass, red snapper, eel, and haddock or cod, or whatever is locally available and absolutely fresh, will nevertheless do very well. Cut the fish, carefully cleaned, and the lobsters, live, into 2-inch pieces, put the coarser-fleshed fish in the kettle first, then the lobsters, then the rest of the fish. Add ¾ cup of dry white wine and boiling water just to cover the fish. Bring the liquid back to a boil and cook the *bouillabaisse*, covered, over very high heat for 15 minutes. If mussels are available, add about 1 pint of them, thoroughly scrubbed, 6 minutes before cooking time is up. Serve in soup plates, from a tureen, with sliced French bread spread with garlic butter and toasted. Or serve the broth poured over the toasted bread and the fish in a separate dish. Serves eight.

TOUR DE CHOIZEL, NEAR MENDE   *Languedoc*

Braised Celery

Céleri Ménagère

(Celery, bacon, onion, carrot, herbs, chicken consommé, butter)

Remove the green outside stalks from 2 heads of celery, cut off the tops below the leaves, trim the root end, and split the heads lengthwise into halves or quarters, depending on their size. Wash them thoroughly and parboil them for 10 minutes. In an ovenproof casserole just large enough to hold the celery in one closely-packed layer, place 1 strip of bacon, diced, and 1 small carrot and 1 onion, both thinly sliced. Arrange the celery, well-drained, on top and add a *bouquet garni,* including a few celery leaves. Add enough clear chicken consommé barely to cover and bring it to a boil. Then place the casserole, covered, in a 350° oven for about 1½ hours, or until the celery is tender, basting occasionally. Remove the celery to a hot platter and keep it warm. Strain the juice in the casserole into a small saucepan, add a lump of butter, and reduce it over high heat for a few minutes. Pour this sauce over the celery and garnish it with chopped parsley and the sliced carrot. Serves four to six.

THE BANKS OF THE RIVER ISÈRE—GRENOBLE *Dauphiny*

Trout Grenoble

Truite à la Grenobloise

(Trout, and a sauce of butter, mushrooms, bread crumbs, lemon, capers)

Clean, wash and dry small fresh trout, trim off the fins, but leave the heads and tails. Sauté them *meunière* by dipping them lightly in flour seasoned with salt and pepper, then browning them on both sides in a heavy skillet with a good tablespoon of hot butter for each fish. Remove them to a hot platter. For 4 small trout add another tablespoon of butter to the skillet and in it sauté 4 minced mushrooms and a heaping tablespoon of bread crumbs. Add the juice of half a lemon and a teaspon of drained capers, stir the sauce briskly for a few seconds and pour it over the trout.

172

SPRINGTIME ROAD NEAR DIE   *Dauphiny*

Guinea Hen Chasseur

Pintade Chasseur

(Guinea hen, herbs, brandy, mushrooms, shallot, garlic, bacon, stock)

Wipe a 2½-pound guinea hen inside and out with a damp cloth and rub the cavity with a mixture of ⅛ teaspoon of dried thyme, 2 or 3 chopped rosemary leaves, ½ teaspoon of olive oil and ½ teaspoon of brandy. Leave these seasonings in the bird and let it stand for several hours.

Make a stuffing with the liver of the guinea hen, 5 large mushrooms, ½ shallot, 1 good sprig of parsley and 6 or 8 fresh rosemary leaves, all chopped, ½ clove of garlic, minced, and salt and freshly ground pepper. Stuff the bird and truss it. Blanch 1 tablespoon of diced bacon in boiling water for 30 seconds and drain it. Melt 1 tablespoon of butter in an iron *cocotte,* add the bacon, and put in the bird. Turn it several times to brown it on all sides, then add ½ cup of chicken stock or consommé. Bake the guinea hen, covered, in a 350° oven for 45 minutes, basting it several times; then remove the cover and let the bird brown for another 15 minutes. Shortly before servingtime, sauté a dozen small mushroom caps in a little olive oil and add a soupçon of shallot and garlic for the last minute of cooking. Season the mushrooms with salt and pepper, sprinkle them with minced parsley and use them to garnish the *pintade*. Serves two or three.

173

FARMHOUSE IN THE MIDI *Languedoc*

Cabbage-stuffed Cabbage

Chou Farci Aristide

(Cabbage, butter, onion, parsley, bread crumbs, eggs, nutmeg)

Discard the wilted outside leaves of a 1½-pound cabbage, and peel off 5 perfect leaves and reserve them. Core the cabbage, and slice and chop the rest of it finely. In a heavy casserole melt 6 tablespoons of butter, add the cabbage and cook it, uncovered, stirring often, over very low heat for 30 minutes, or until it is soft and golden. Add 1 medium onion, minced, and 1 tablespoon of chopped parsley, and simmer all together for 10 minutes. Let the cabbage cool, add 3 tablespoons of bread crumbs, 2 lightly beaten eggs, a pinch of nutmeg, and salt and pepper, and mix well. Put a clean cloth in a bowl, leaving the edges hanging over the side. Arrange the reserved cabbage leaves in the bowl, overlapping and stem ends up, to form a large cup closed at the bottom. Spoon the cabbage into this cup, pull the cloth up around it and tie it tightly, like a pudding in a bag. Drop the "pudding" into boiling salted water to cover generously, and cook it at the lowest possible simmer for 1 hour, turning it once. Unwrap it, drain it, and put it in a serving bowl, stem end down, with a little melted butter poured over it. To serve, quarter the cabbage with a sharp knife. Serves four.

174

VILLAGE TOOL SHOP *Guyenne*

Rice and Vegetable Salad

Salade de Riz

(Rice, green beans, artichoke bottoms, celery, eggs, radishes, French dressing)

Boil 1 cup of rice in plenty of salted water until it is done but still quite firm. Drain it thoroughly and while it is still hot add ¼ cup of tart French dressing made of 2 parts wine vinegar, 5 parts olive oil, and salt and pepper to taste. When the rice has cooled, mix with it ¾ cup of diced cooked green beans, 3 cooked and diced artichoke bottoms (canned if you wish), 1 small stalk of celery with its leaves, finely chopped, and the whites of 3 hard-boiled eggs, also finely chopped. Turn the salad into a glass bowl, sprinkle the top with the sieved yolks of the 3 hard-boiled eggs, and decorate it with thinly sliced red radishes and a circle of minced parsley. To serve, add another ¼ cup of French dressing and toss the salad again at the table. This is excellent with cold chicken or cold boiled lobster. Serves four.

LES SABLES D'OLONNES   *Poitou*

Poached Fish with Black-butter and Caper Sauce
Raie au Beurre Noir
(Fish, onion, herbs, vinegar, capers, butter)

The French use black-butter and caper sauce to glorify the otherwise un-
interesting skate, or *raie*. This fish is not often found in our markets, but a sauce
au beurre noir also improves many other fish that are of sturdy texture and flavor,
such as cod, haddock or halibut.

Place a 3-pound piece of fish in a saucepan, sprinkle it with salt and pepper,
and add 1 small onion, sliced, 1 bay leaf, a pinch of thyme, ¼ cup of vinegar,
and enough water barely to cover. Bring the liquid to a boil and poach the fish,
covered, over the lowest possible heat for about 20 minutes, or until it is firm.
Put it on a cloth to drain, skin it, and take out the bones that can be removed
without breaking it. Transfer the fish to a hot platter and sprinkle it with
chopped parsley and 4 teaspoons of drained capers. Meanwhile, melt ¼ pound of
butter in a skillet, heat it slowly until it is dark brown, and pour it over the
fish. Stir 3 tablespoons of vinegar into the hot skillet, pour this over the butter
sauce and serve immediately. Serves six.

MOUNTAIN VILLAGE *Pyrenees*

Stuffed Baked Tomatoes

Tomates Farcies

(Tomatoes, sausage meat, bread crumbs, onion, garlic, parsley, butter)

Slice off and reserve the smooth ends of 4 firm tomatoes. Scoop out the centers of the tomatoes, reserve them, and discard the seeds. Mix together a stuffing of ¼ pound of fresh sausage meat, ½ cup of bread crumbs moistened with 2 table-spoons of consommé, 1 small onion and 1 small clove of garlic, both minced and sautéed together in butter until soft, the tomato centers, chopped, and 2 table-spoons of chopped parsley. Stuff the tomatoes, sprinkle them with fine bread crumbs, dot each one with a small piece of butter, replace the caps, and bake them in a lightly oiled baking dish in a 300° oven for 35 minutes. Serves four.

MALMAISON   *Ile-de-France*

King Henry IV's "Chicken for Every Pot"
Poule au Pot Henri IV

(Fowl, bread, ham, shallots, garlic, herbs, eggs, carrots, turnips, onions, leeks)

Use a plump 5- to 6-pound boiling fowl. Mix together well a stuffing of 5 slices of stale French bread, crumbled and soaked in ½ cup of milk; the liver, heart and skinned giblet of the hen, and 1 slice of ham or bacon, all ground together with the finest blade of a meat grinder; 2 shallots and 2 cloves of garlic, all minced; 2 tablespoons of chopped parsley and a pinch each of rosemary, thyme, nutmeg, salt and pepper; and lastly, 2 small eggs, or 1 large one, lightly beaten. Stuff the hen, sew it up carefully at both ends, and truss it.

Put the hen in a soup kettle and add 3 small carrots and 2 small white turnips, all cut in pieces; 3 whole onions, one of them stuck with 2 cloves; 2 leeks with most of the green part cut off; 1 small stalk of celery with its leaves; and 1 bay leaf, 6 crushed peppercorns, and 1 teaspoon of salt. Add water to cover the hen, but not more than 3 quarts. Cover the kettle and bring the water to a boil, then simmer the hen over very low heat for 2 hours, or until it is tender. To serve, carve the hen and arrange the meat on a hot platter. Break open the carcass, remove the stuffing and slice it. Arrange the stuffing and the vegetables around the meat, pour a little of the broth over the platter, and serve the rest in cups. Coarse salt is passed at the table with *poule au pot*. Serves six.

178

LANDSCAPE NEAR VIENNE   *Dauphiny*

Hot Apple Mousse

Mousse de Pommes

(Apples, butter, sugar, egg whites, apricot jam, kirsch)

Peel, quarter and core 2 pounds of tart apples. Bake them, covered with a piece of heavily buttered paper, buttered side down, in a 350° oven for 45 minutes, stirring them occasionally. Force the apples through a sieve, add ⅓ cup of sugar, simmer them until they are thick and jamlike, stirring often, and let them cool. Meanwhile, in a saucepan over medium heat melt ½ cup of sugar and heat it, stirring constantly, until it turns golden brown. Coat the inside of a 1½-quart soufflé mold with this caramel and let it harden. Beat 6 egg whites stiff with 3 tablespoons of sugar and fold them into the applesauce. Spoon the apple mousse into the mold and bake it in a pan of hot water, on a low rack in a 350° oven, for 1¼ hours. Let it cool for 15 minutes, then unmold it onto a platter. Serve warm, with a hot sauce made of 1½ cups of apricot jam puréed in an electric blender, thinned with a little water if necessary, and flavored with 2 teaspoons of kirsch. Serves six.

MANOIR DU LIEU-BINET, NEAR LISIEUX *Normandy*

Normandy Scalloped Potatoes

Pommes Gratinées à la Normande

(Potatoes, leeks, onion, butter, bay leaf, chicken stock)

In a skillet sauté the white parts of 2 leeks and 1 medium onion, all thinly sliced, in 2 tablespoons of hot butter until they are soft and golden but not at all brown. Slice 4 large potatoes thinly, arrange a third of the slices in a buttered baking dish, spread half the sautéed vegetables over them, put in another third of the potatoes, then the rest of the vegetables and 1 bay leaf, and finish with the rest of the potatoes. (Sprinkle a little pepper between layers, but no salt.) Fill the dish just to the level of the top layer of potatoes with chicken stock or consommé, dot the *gratin* generously with butter, and bake it in a very slow oven for 1¼ to 1½ hours, or until the potatoes are done, the liquid is absorbed and the top is delicately browned. Serves four.

180

MONT ST. MICHEL   *Normandy*

Braised Peas and Carrots

Carottes et Petits Pcis à l'Etuvée

(Carrots, peas, butter, onion, herbs)

Scrape and dice 6 young carrots. Simmer them in a heavy saucepan, covered, for 10 minutes, with ½ cup of water, a good lump of butter, 1 small onion, sliced, a pinch each of sugar and thyme, and salt and pepper. Then add 2 cups of green peas, ½ cup of water and a sprig of parsley, and cook the vegetables together slowly, still covered, until they are tender, or for about 20 minutes. The water should be almost all evaporated when the vegetables are done. Serves four.

181

CLUNY MUSEUM   *Paris*

Poached Peaches with Raspberry Sauce

Pêches aux Framboises Antoinette

(Fresh peaches and raspberries, sugar, vanilla bean, kirsch)

Parboil 8 ripe peaches, preferably white cling-stone peaches, in boiling water
for 1 minute, peel them and leave them whole. In a saucepan boil together 1½
cups of water, ¾ cup of granulated sugar and a piece of vanilla bean for 3 or 4
minutes. Remove the vanilla bean, poach the peaches in the syrup over low heat
for 5 minutes, and remove them to a serving bowl. In an electric blender, purée
3 cups of fresh raspberries and strain out the seeds through a fine sieve. Sweeten
the sauce to taste with 2 or 3 tablespoons of the peach syrup and add 2 teaspoons of kirsch. Pour it over the peaches, chill the fruit before serving, and
garnish it with slivered blanched almonds. Serves four to six.

182

THE TOWN OF MONTBARD   *Burgundy*

Braised Ham with Mushroom Sauce

Saulpiquet Montbardois Belin

(Half a ham, seasonings, white wine, stock, mushrooms, cream, peas, lemon, brandy)

Trim the fat from a 5-pound half of a processed ham. (Or use half a smoked ham, but simmer it in water first, allowing 15 minutes per pound.) In a heavy saucepan or kettle brown lightly in butter 1 small carrot and 1 onion, both sliced. Put in the prepared ham, a *bouquet garni,* and 2 cups each of dry white wine, chicken stock or consommé, and water. Braise the ham, covered, at the lowest possible simmer, allowing 15 minutes per pound, and turn it once while it is cooking. When it is done, let it rest in the liquid for 15 minutes, then remove it and keep it warm.

Skim all the fat from the broth and simmer it briskly until it is reduced by about one third. Sauté ¾ pound of sliced fresh mushrooms in 2½ tablespoons of butter for 5 minutes. Dissolve 1 tablespoon of potato flour in a little of the reduced ham broth, then add enough broth to make 1¾ cups. Add this to the mushrooms, add 1¼ cups of heavy cream, and simmer the sauce for 5 minutes, stirring often. Then add 1 cup of cooked young green peas, 2 tablespoons of brandy, and the juice of half a lemon, and simmer another 2 or 3 minutes. Serve the ham carved into thin slices with the sauce poured over them. Serves eight.

183

MINIATURE PORT AT STE. MARINE   *Brittany*

Lobster Canapés
Canapés Bretonne
(Lobster, mayonnaise, lemon juice, white bread, parsley, capers)

Carefully remove the tail meat of large boiled lobsters, and remove the coral, if any, and the green tomalley. Save the shells and the rest of the meat for some other purpose, such as a bisque (see *Index*). With a very sharp knife split the tail meat lengthwise and cut it crosswise into neat slices.

Season homemade mayonnaise to taste with plenty of lemon juice, white pepper and the tomalley (about 3 parts mayonnaise to 1 part tomalley). Spread thin 1½-inch circles of firm white bread with the seasoned mayonnaise and top each canapé with a slice of lobster. Decorate with a tiny sprig of parsley and with a scrap of the scarlet coral or a caper. Serve the canapés as soon as possible, but meanwhile cover them with aluminum foil and keep them in a cool place.

184

THE LOWER GARDENS—VERSAILLES *Ile-de-France*

Pheasant with Endive

Faisan aux Endives

(Pheasant, salt pork, onion, carrot, chicken consommé, endives, lemon)

Tie a strip of salt pork over the breast of a cleaned and trussed 3½-pound pheasant. In a flameproof casserole brown the bird on all sides in 2 tablespoons of hot butter. Add 1 onion and 1 small carrot, both quartered, and ½ cup of chicken consommé, lower the heat, and cook the pheasant for 50 minutes. Put a piece of parchment paper under the lid to catch the steam, discard this liquid occasionally, and add more consommé sparingly to the casserole as needed. Ten minutes before the bird is done, turn it breast side down to finish browning. Meanwhile, slice 8 heads of endive crosswise into ¾-inch sections, separate the leaves, and heat them slowly in a heavy saucepan with 2 tablespoons of melted butter. When they begin to soften, add salt and pepper, the juice of 1 lemon, and ½ cup of water, and simmer the endive until it is cooked through and the liquid is almost evaporated. When the pheasant is done, transfer it to a hot platter and discard the trussing strings and the salt pork. Stir ¼ cup of boiling water into the juices in the casserole, scrape up all the brown scraps, strain this sauce over the bird, and add the endive to the platter. Serves four.

185

LOCKSMITH SHOP—OBERNAI *Alsace*

Alsatian Ham and Beef Broth
Bouillon à l'Alsacienne

(Ham bone, soup beef or canned broth, vegetables, herbs, cabbage, leek, potatoes)

In a soup kettle put a ham bone with a little meat on it, a 1½-pound piece of soup beef, and 2½ quarts of unsalted water. Bring the water to a boil slowly and skim it carefully just before it begins to bubble. Then add 1 stalk of celery with its leaves, 1 onion and 1 carrot, all cut in pieces, 6 crushed peppercorns, 1 bay leaf and a sprig of parsley. Cover the kettle and simmer the broth over the lowest possible heat for 2½ hours, skimming occasionally. Remove the ham bone and meat, strain the broth through a colander lined with a cloth, cool it, then skim off the fat. To serve, add ½ cup each of finely shredded cabbage and leeks, first parboiled until tender but still slightly crisp, and 1 cup of diced boiled potatoes. Reheat the soup and add salt if necessary. This makes 1½ to 2 quarts of bouillon. The same soup can be made by boiling the ham bone alone, with the same seasonings, in 1½ quarts of water. Add 3 cups of canned beef broth 15 minutes before the cooking time is up.

186

SPRINGTIME VALLEY, NEAR MARLENS   *Savoy*

Strawberries and Cream

Fraises en Vasque

(Strawberries, sugar, cherry brandy, cream, sour cream, pistachio nuts)

Wash and drain very thoroughly 3 pints of large perfect strawberries, hull them and put them in a glass serving bowl. Sprinkle them lightly with granulated sugar, add 2 tablespoons of cherry brandy, and chill them for several hours. Just before servingtime, with a whisk beat 1 cup of heavy cream until it thickens a little, but do not whip it, and blend it with ½ cup of thick sour cream. This will approximate the wonderful *crème fraîche* which is unobtainable in America. Pour the cream over the berries and sprinkle it with chopped pistachio nuts. Serves six to eight.

187

CHÂTEAU BY THE RIVER—BOURDEILLES *Périgord*

Veal Marengo

Veau Sauté Marengo

(Veal, olive oil, tomatoes, onions, white wine, stock, garlic, mushrooms)

Whether or not Napoleon actually was regaled with *veau sauté Marengo* on the battle fields of Italy, its fame promises to be as lasting as that of the little emperor himself.

In a heavy casserole brown 1½ pounds of tender stewing veal, cut in cubes, in 3 tablespoons of olive oil. Add 4 ripe tomatoes, peeled, seeded and chopped, and 1 dozen tiny whole onions (2 medium onions, coarsely chopped, will do) first browned briefly in butter. Simmer the mixture for 4 or 5 minutes, sprinkle on 2 teaspoons of flour and blend it in thoroughly. Then add 1 cup of dry white wine, 2 cups of chicken stock or consommé, 1 whole clove of garlic, and salt and pepper. Cover the casserole and simmer the veal for 1 hour. Then add 1 dozen mushroom caps, first sautéed for 3 or 4 minutes in butter, and simmer all together for another ½ hour, or until the meat is tender. Serve sprinkled with chopped parsley and garnished with sautéed croutons. Serves four.

THE CHÂTEAU AT FLEURY-EN-BIÈRE *Ile-de-France*

Puréed Apricots and Cream

Abricots Chantilly

(Dried apricots, sugar, almonds, whipped cream)

Rinse a 14-ounce package of dried apricots, put them in a saucepan with water to cover well, and simmer them very slowly, uncovered, for 25 minutes. Then stir in ½ cup of granulated sugar and cook them another 5 minutes. Force the stewed apricots through a colander, or cool them and purée them in an electric blender. Mix ¼ cup of blanched slivered almonds into the purée, spoon it into a glass serving bowl and chill.

Just before servingtime, whip ¾ cup of cream, flavor it with a little sugar and vanilla and spread it over the apricots. Or the whipped cream may be mixed into the cooled apricot purée along with the almonds, making a sort of mousse which should be chilled in individual *pots de crème*.

THE LOWER TOWN—DINAN *Brittany*

Sole (or Flounder) Meunière

Sole Meunière

(Sole or flounder, flour, butter, lemon juice, parsley)

A small, whole, and very nearly unobtainable Dover sole is the ideal fish to sauté *meunière*. However, the many American varieties of sole and flounder, whole or filleted, are also at their best when treated in this perfectly simple fashion.

Sprinkle the fish lightly with salt and pepper, dip it in flour and shake off the excess. Melt enough butter in a skillet to coat the surface generously, but not an excessive amount. Put in the fish as soon as the butter is hot and sizzling, but before it starts to brown. Lower the heat, cook the fish slowly for 5 minutes, turn it, and brown the other side for 5 minutes. Fillets and small whole fish will then be golden brown and cooked through, but larger pieces will have to be turned again to cook for another 2 or 3 minutes on each side. Remove the fish to a hot platter when it is done, sprinkle generously with lemon juice and chopped parsley, and keep it warm. For each serving add 1 generous tablespoon of butter to the skillet, and heat it until it is dark gold and foaming but not brown. Pour the hot butter over the fish, garnish each piece with a slice of lemon dipped in minced parsley, and serve immediately.

190

REMAINS OF THE ROMAN THEATER—ARLES   *Provence*

Country Roast Pork with Herbs
Rôti de Porc Campagnarde
(Boned pork roast, herbs, white wine)

This is a standard method applicable to any cut of pork suitable for roasting. The piece need not be boned, but the herbs are more effective if it is. Cuts with a heavy layer of fat should be partly trimmed and scored with a sharp knife.

For a roast weighing 2 pounds after boning, crush together to a powder, preferably in a mortar, 2 tablespoons of coarse salt, ½ teaspoon of dried thyme, ½ teaspoon of mixed powdered clove, cinnamon and nutmeg, 1 bay leaf, and a dozen peppercorns. Rub the meat well on all sides and in every crevice with this powder, then roll and tie it if necessary. Let it stand in a cool place for 24 hours. Roast it, uncovered, in a 350° oven for 1½ hours. turning it occasionally and basting it often, first with a little hot water and later with the accumulated pan juices. When the roast is done, remove it to a hot platter and garnish it with water cress. Skim as much fat as possible from the pan juices and stir into them ⅓ cup each of hot water and dry white wine. Scrape up all the brown scraps, simmer the sauce for 2 or 3 minutes, strain it, and serve it in a sauce boat. Mashed potatoes are the natural accompaniment. Serves four.

HILLSIDE STREET—CHAUMONT-EN-VEXIN   *Ile-de-France*

Chicken Consommé Velouté

Consommé Velouté

(Chicken consommé, potato starch, egg yolks, fresh tarragon)

Use 7 cups of chicken consommé in all. Bring 6 cups of the consommé just to the boiling point. Blend smoothly 2 tablespoons of potato starch with ½ cup of cold consommé and, with a wire whisk, stir the mixture slowly into the hot soup. Simmer it, uncovered, for 15 minutes, then let it cool. Shortly before servingtime, mix 4 egg yolks with another ½ cup of cold consommé and stir them carefully into the soup with the whisk. Reheat the soup, stirring and being sure not to let it boil, until it begins to thicken. If you can get them, float fresh tarragon leaves on each serving of *velouté*. Serves six to eight.

CANAL BARGE—NEAR BRIENNON *Lyonnais*

Fish Sauté Romagnole

Poisson à la Paysanne Romagnole

(Fish sautéed in a sauce of olive oil, garlic, tomatoes, white wine, herbs)

In a heavy casserole sauté gently 2 cloves of garlic and 1 tablespoon of parsley, all finely minced, in 4 tablespoons of olive oil. Add 3 pounds of any firm white fish (halibut, haddock, whitefish, carp or pickerel, for instance) cut in 2-inch pieces. Sauté the fish over a low flame for 5 minutes, being careful not to let it stick. Add 4 large, ripe tomatoes, peeled, seeded and chopped (or 1½ cups of drained Italian plum tomatoes), ¼ cup of dry white wine, salt, pepper, and a good pinch of thyme. Cover the casserole and simmer the fish for 20 minutes, or until the tomatoes are reduced to a juicy but flavorful sauce. Serve with boiled new potatoes. Serves six.

193

CHÂTEAU DE RIGNY-USSÉ   *Touraine*

Chicken en Cocotte

Poulet en Cocotte

(Chicken, bacon, butter, onions, carrots, white wine, mushrooms)

In a flameproof casserole brown 1 strip of bacon, finely diced, in 1 tablespoon of hot butter. Remove the bacon, reserve it, and put a cleaned and trussed 4-pound chicken on its side in the casserole. Brown it on one side, then the other, then breast down, for 5 minutes each time. Meanwhile, in a skillet sauté a second strip of diced bacon in 1 tablespoon of butter, remove it and set it aside. To the fat remaining in the skillet add 8 to 10 tiny whole onions, or 3 or 4 medium ones, quartered, and 3 medium carrots, cut in small pieces. Toss the vegetables in the fat, sprinkle them with ½ tablespoon of sugar, and cook them, stirring often, until they are brown on all sides, or about 10 minutes. Then turn the chicken on its back, and add to the casserole the sautéed vegetables, salt, pepper, ½ cup of hot water, and ¼ cup of dry white wine. Place it, uncovered, in a 350° oven and bake the chicken for 45 minutes to 1 hour. Fifteen minutes before it is done, add the reserved bacon and ¼ pound of quartered mushrooms first sautéed briefly in a little butter. Sprinkle the *poulet en cocotte* with chopped parsley and serve it from the casserole with sautéed potato balls.

194

THE LOUVRE FROM THE SEINE   *Paris*

Parisian Madeleines

Madeleines

(Eggs, sugar, flour, butter, lemon rind)

In the top of a double boiler, over barely simmering water, work together with a wooden spoon 4 lightly beaten eggs and ½ cup of fine granulated sugar until the mixture is creamy and lukewarm. Take it from the heat and beat it again until it is cold. Beat in gradually 1⅛ cups of flour, sifted after measuring, ½ cup of lukewarm melted butter, and the grated rind of 1 small lemon. Butter and flour lightly small shell-shaped Madeleine molds, or fluted tartlet molds, and fill them two-thirds full of batter. Bake the Madeleines in a 400° oven for 25 minutes. Makes a dozen or more small Madeleines.

LA ROQUE-GAGEAC ON THE DORDOGNE *Dordogne*

Blanquette of Lamb Gascony

Agneau en Blanquette à la Gasconne

(Lamb, ham, onion, herbs, lemon juice, egg yolks)

In an iron *cocotte* heat 1 tablespoon of butter and in it brown quickly 2 pounds of good lean stewing lamb, cut in cubes. Add 1 cup of finely diced ham, 2 onions, chopped, a *bouquet garni,* and boiling water to cover. Put the lid on the *cocotte* and simmer the stew for 2 hours. Then, in a small bowl, blend 1 tablespoon of flour with ¼ cup of the cooking liquid, add this to the stew and let it simmer another ½ hour.

Shortly before servingtime, drain the cooking liquid into a bowl, discard the *bouquet garni,* and keep the meat hot in a covered dish. In a saucepan mix 2 egg yolks with 2 teaspoons of lemon juice, then stir in slowly 2½ cups of the hot stock. Reheat this sauce cautiously, stirring constantly and not letting it boil, until it is slightly thickened. Pour it over the lamb and serve the *blanquette* with steamed new potatoes. Serves four.

NOTRE-DAME AND THE ILE ST. LOUIS   *Paris*

Parisian Gnocchis
Gnocchis Parisienne

(Butter, flour, eggs, Swiss cheese, dry mustard, cayenne, cream sauce)

Add ¼ teaspoon of salt and 2 tablespoons of butter to 1½ cups of water and bring the mixture to a boil in a small saucepan. Take the pan off the fire and beat in 1½ cups of flour, sifted after measuring. When the mixture is smooth, beat in 3 large eggs, one at a time, and continue beating until the dough is shiny. Then mix in 3 tablespoons of grated Swiss cheese, 1 teaspoon of dry mustard, salt to taste, and a touch of cayenne.

Heat a large saucepan of salted water barely to the boiling point. Dip a teaspoon in the hot water to heat it, scoop up a small piece of the *gnocchi* paste with it and scoop it out again, with another heated spoon, into the simmering, never boiling, water. Poach the miniature dumplings for about 15 minutes, or until they are just firm. Take them carefully from the water with a slotted spoon as they are done, drain them on a clean cloth, and then arrange them in a shallow buttered baking dish. Cover the *gnocchis* with 1½ cups of cream sauce made with thin cream and seasoned with salt, cayenne and 3 tablespoons of grated cheese. Sprinkle the dish with a little more cheese, dot with butter and glaze briefly under a hot broiler. Serves four.

ABBAYE DE SOLESMES   *Maine*

Crème Brulée

Crème Brulée à la Jeanne

(Heavy cream, eggs, dark brown sugar)

Scald 2 cups of heavy cream in the top of a double boiler. In a bowl beat together with an egg beater 4 eggs, a pinch of salt and 3 tablespoons of dark brown sugar. Pour the hot cream slowly into the beaten eggs, stirring constantly, and return the mixture to the double boiler. Cook the custard for exactly 3 minutes over simmering water, beating constantly with the egg beater. Pour the custard into an ovenproof serving dish and let it cool completely. Then cover the top with a ¼-inch layer of finely crumbled dark brown sugar and put the custard under a hot broiler, leaving the door open, until the sugar melts and glazes. Chill the *crème brulée* for several hours and serve it ice cold. Serves six.

THE GRAND' PLACE—ARRAS   *Flanders*

Asparagus with Egg and Butter Sauce

Asperge à la Flamande

(Asparagus, hard-boiled eggs, parsley, lemon juice, butter)

Boil 1 pound of asparagus, washed, scraped and trimmed, in salted water for 20 minutes, or until it is tender but still firm. Drain the asparagus first in a colander, then on a clean cloth. Arrange it on a hot platter and sprinkle the tips with the mashed yolks, still warm, of 4 hard-boiled eggs, 2 tablespoons of minced parsley, and the juice of half a lemon. Pour over this ¼ cup of melted butter, heated until golden but not brown, garnish the platter with quarters of lemon, and serve immediately. Serves four.

CATHEDRAL OF ST. PIERRE—BEAUVAIS   *Ile-de-France*

Jellied Beef Tongue

Langue de Boeuf en Gelée

(Beef tongue, veal knuckle, onions, carrots, herbs, spices, white wine, brandy)

Boil a well-scrubbed fresh tongue in lightly salted water to cover for 1 hour, skimming the surface several times. Remove the tongue, skin it and trim off the roots. In an ovenproof casserole brown lightly 2 onions and 2 carrots, all cut in pieces, in 1 tablespoon of bacon fat. Add the prepared tongue, a cracked veal knuckle, a *bouquet garni,* 1 clove of garlic, 6 whole cloves, 6 crushed peppercorns, 1 teaspoon of salt, ½ cup of dry white wine, and 4 cups of the water in which the tongue was boiled. Cook the tongue, tightly covered, in a 250° oven for 2 hours, or until it is tender.

Remove the tongue, cool it, and store it in the refrigerator. Strain the broth through a cloth, reserving the carrots, and simmer it until it is reduced to 3 cups. Cool it and store it also in the refrigerator. Next day, or when the broth has jelled firmly, scrape off all the fat, bring the broth to a boil, add 1 ounce of brandy, simmer it another minute and take it off the heat. Slice the tongue and arrange the slices in a serving dish, sprinkle them with minced parsley and garnish them with slices of the reserved carrots. Pour on the broth, let the dish cool, and chill it until the broth has jelled again.

200

CHÂTEAU DE CHAUMONT, ON THE LOIRE *Orléanais*

Baked Salmon Val de Loire

Saumon Val de Loire

(Salmon, salt pork or bacon, shallots, butter, wine vinegar, white wine)

Skin one side of a 2-pound piece of salmon. Tie a slice of bacon over the skinned side; or better, with a larding needle run a few fine strips of salt pork into the fish. Butter a shallow baking dish, put in 3 or 4 minced shallots and place the salmon on top of them, skin side down. Dot the fish with 4 tablespoons of butter and bake it, uncovered, in a 350° oven for 15 minutes, basting several times with the pan juices. The add ¼ cup each of good wine vinegar and water to the pan, and cook the fish another 15 minutes, still basting. Remove the salmon to a hot platter, discard the bacon, and keep the fish warm. On top of the stove, dilute the pan juices with ½ cup of dry white wine and stir in 1 tablespoon of butter creamed with 2 teaspoons of flour. Simmer the sauce, stirring often, for 2 or 3 minutes, taste it for seasoning, strain it, and pour it over the salmon. Serves four.

VINEGROWN COTTAGE—ALBIGNY   *Savoy*

Baked Eggs Savoy

Flan d'Oeufs sur le Plat Savoyarde

(Eggs, cream, nutmeg, butter, grated cheese)

Separate 6 eggs, putting the whites in a bowl and leaving each yolk in half an egg shell. With an egg beater, beat the whites with ¼ cup of heavy cream, a pinch of nutmeg, and salt and pepper, until the mixture is frothy. In a shallow baking dish, over low heat and using an asbestos mat, put 2 tablespoons of butter and add the egg whites as soon as it melts. Cook them, stirring constantly with a whisk, until they are thick and creamy. Take the dish from the fire and drop the yolks one by one in a circle on top of the whites. Cover the baking dish, put it back on the fire, still using the mat, and cook the eggs for about 6 minutes, or until the whites are puffed and set but still soft. Serve the *flan* immediately, from the baking dish, with mild freshly grated cheese to sprinkle over it and accompanied by a crisp green salad with a tart dressing. Serves three or four.

STREET CORNER, BAR-SUR-SEINE   *Champagne*

Blanquette of Turkey

Blanquette de Dindon à la Crème

(Cold roast turkey, butter, flour, cream, turkey broth, mushrooms, lemon juice)

Cut cold roast turkey into large dice and remove the skin. For 2 packed cups of turkey meat, blend 1 tablespoon of flour into 1½ tablespoons of melted butter and add gradually ½ cup each of thin cream and turkey broth made from the carcass (or use canned chicken consommé). Add salt and pepper to taste and cook the sauce, stirring often, until it is smooth and slightly thickened. Meanwhile, in a small covered saucepan, simmer ¼ pound of quartered mushrooms for 5 minutes in 3 tablespoons of water and 1 tablespoon of lemon juice. Add the turkey meat and the mushrooms, with their liquor, to the cream sauce, and simmer the *blanquette* slowly until the turkey is heated through. Serves four.

ORNANS ON THE RIVER LOUE

Franche-Comté

Lentil Soup Conti

Purée de Lentilles à la Conti

(Lentils, bacon, butter, onion, carrot, herbs, egg yolks, croutons or lemon)

Soak 1 cup of lentils in cold water overnight. Drain them and put them in a soup kettle with 6 cups of fresh water and 1 teaspoon of salt. Bring the water to a boil and skim the surface once or twice. Meanwhile, in a skillet, sauté 2 strips of bacon, diced, in 1 tablespoon of butter. Add 1 onion and 1 carrot, both chopped, and a pinch of thyme. Simmer all together over a low flame for 7 or 8 minutes until the vegetables are golden but not brown. Add 1 bay leaf, 2 sprigs of parsley and the contents of the skillet to the simmering lentils. Cover the kettle and simmer the soup for 2½ hours, or until the lentils are thoroughly cooked. Then remove the parsley and bay leaf and force the soup through a sieve; or cool it and purée it in an electric blender. To serve, mix a little of the soup in the bottom of a tureen with 2 lightly beaten egg yolks. Reheat the soup, taste it for seasoning, and pour it into the tureen. Stir it carefully and garnish it with small croutons sautéed in butter, or with thin slices of lemon. Serves four.

204

THE PORT—VILLEFRANCHE-SUR-MER *Riviera*

Garlic-broiled Lobster

Homard Grillé à l'Ail

(Lobster, butter, garlic, parsley, mayonnaise, sour cream, lemon juice)

Split live lobsters lengthwise and remove the intestinal veins. Crack the claws, lay the lobsters flat, shell side down, in a broiler pan, and butter the meat with a little Burgundian snail butter (see *Index*). Broil the lobsters under a high flame, but not too close to it, for 15 to 20 minutes depending on their size, and slip a little more snail butter into each shell as soon as the meat pulls away from it. Serve the lobsters immediately, with a chilled sauce made of 3 parts homemade mayonnaise thinned with 1 part sour cream and seasoned with a touch of crushed garlic and lemon juice.

SUNSET ON THE RHÔNE   *Lyonnais*

Onion Omelette with Croutons

Omelette Lyonnaise aux Croûtons

(Eggs, butter, onions, bread, wine vinegar)

In a skillet sauté 2 medium white onions, thinly sliced, in a generous table-spoon of butter until they are soft and golden. In a second skillet sauté ¼ cup of finely diced white bread in butter, stirring often, until it is brown and crisp. Make a 6-egg omelette and when it is set but still soft, take it off the fire, spread the onions across the center, sprinkle the croutons over the onions, fold the omelette and turn it out on a platter. Melt and brown slightly 1 more tablespoon of butter in one of the skillets, stir in ½ teaspoon of wine vinegar and pour this over the omelette. Serves three or four.

OLD SALTS OF CONCARNEAU   *Brittany*

Mussels (or Clams) Marinière
Moules Marinière

(Mussels, white wine, onions, garlic, parsley, thyme, butter)

Though fresh mussels are not as hard to find in the fish markets as they once were, they do remain scarce; clams, particularly the soft-shelled ones, can be substituted with a different but no less worthy result.

Brush, scrape and wash thoroughly 2 quarts of mussels. Put them in a soup kettle with ½ cup of dry white wine, 2 white onions (or 3 shallots) and 1 clove of garlic, all minced, ¼ cup of chopped parsley, a pinch of thyme, and freshly ground pepper, but no salt. Cook them, covered, over a brisk flame, shaking them several times. The mussels are done when the shells have opened, or in about 6 minutes. Remove them and keep them warm, and pour into a saucepan as much of the cooking liquid as you can without taking the sand that will probably be in the bottom. Add 3 tablespoons of butter creamed with 1 teaspoon of flour, and reduce the sauce quickly for 3 or 4 minutes. Serve the mussels in soup plates and pour the sauce over them. Serves four as a first course, two as a main dish.

DRY-GOODS STANDS—ST. FLOUR *Auvergne*

Mushrooms on Toast

Croûtes Bayonnaise

(Mushrooms, bread, butter, ham)

For each serving allow 1 heaping tablespoon of finely diced cooked ham, 4 whole mushrooms and a slice of bread, either good white bread with the crust trimmed off, or a slice of French bread ⅜ inch thick, untrimmed and cut on the diagonal to make it large enough.

Trim the stems from the mushrooms and wash and wipe the caps; do not peel them. In one skillet brown the slices of bread on both sides in plenty of hot butter. Turn the slices at once to coat both sides with butter before browning them; this will keep them from soaking up an exorbitant amount. In another skillet lightly brown the diced ham in a little butter. Remove the ham, add more butter to the skillet and sauté the mushrooms in it. Remove them when they are golden but before they begin to shrivel and arrange them on the croutons. Sprinkle the ham over the mushrooms, season the *croûtes* with freshly ground pepper, and brown them under the broiler for 2 minutes just before serving.

208

HÔTEL DE VILLE—COMPIÈGNE   *Ile-de-France*

Venison Cutlets with Chestnut Purée
Côtelettes de Chevreuil aux Marrons

(Venison cutlets or loin steaks, marinade, Madeira, cream, chestnuts)

Marinate 4 venison cutlets (loin steaks), cut 1½ inches thick, for at least 6 hours in a mixture of 2 tablespoons each of olive oil, dry white wine and wine vinegar, with 1 bay leaf, ½ an onion and 1 clove of garlic, both chopped, and a little thyme, chopped parsley, salt, and freshly ground pepper. Turn the cutlets occasionally and wipe them carefully before cooking them. In a skillet sauté them quickly in a little hot oil for 3 or 4 minutes on each side. They should be brown, but rare inside. Transfer them to a hot platter and keep them warm. Add 2 tablespoons of butter to the skillet, stir in 2 tablespoons of Madeira and ½ cup of cream, and add salt and pepper to taste. Simmer the sauce, stirring, for 1 or 2 minutes, and pour it over the cutlets. Serve them with a chestnut purée made of 1½ pounds of chestnuts, shelled, boiled in salted water with a stalk of celery until tender, carefully peeled, then forced through a sieve, reheated and beaten with a whisk with cream, butter, and salt and pepper. Serves four.

H *   209

ANTIQUE SHOP—COLMAR   *Alsace*

Mocha Cake
Gâteau Moka
(Eggs, sugar, flour, butter, rum, mocha butter-cream, toasted almonds)

In the top of a double boiler beat together with a whisk 6 eggs and ¾ cup of sugar. Continue beating the mixture over barely simmering water until it is creamy and lukewarm. Take it from the heat and beat again until it is cold. Add 2 teaspoons of rum and beat in, still with the whisk, 1¼ cups of flour, sifted after measuring. Stir in ¼ cup of lukewarm melted butter and pour the batter into a buttered and lightly floured 9-inch cake pan. Bake this *génoise* in a 350° oven for 35 minutes and unmold it onto a cake rack to cool.

With a wooden spoon cream thoroughly ¼ pound of butter. Heat 5 tablespoons of sugar dissolved in 2 tablespoons of extremely strong hot coffee until the syrup spins a light thread. With a whisk beat the syrup gradually into 2 lightly beaten egg yolks, and continue beating until the mixture is cool and thickened. Beat this coffee cream into the butter, spread the *crème au beurre* on the cake, and cover the sides with slivered toasted almonds.

HARAS-DU-PIN   *Normandy*

Normandy Potato Salad

Salade Cauchoise

(Potatoes, celery, cream, sour cream, vinegar, lemon juice, ham)

Boil 1 pound of potatoes in their jackets, taking care not to overcook them. Peel them when they are cold and cut them in julienne strips, as for shoe-string potatoes. Cut enough white center stalks of celery, also in julienne strips, to make about half as much celery as potatoes. Whip ¾ cup of heavy cream just long enough to thicken it to the consistency of a thin mayonnaise. Add ¼ cup of sour cream and season well with 2 tablespoons of vinegar, the juice of ½ lemon, or more to taste, and salt and white pepper. Pour this dressing over the salad, mix it in gently so as not to break the potatoes, and turn the salad into a serving dish. Scatter about ½ cup of ham cut in julienne strips over the salad. The incomparable last touch, that is, however, expendable, is 1 or 2 truffles also cut in the same way and added with the ham. Serves four.

211

THE VILLAGE OF ROCHESERVIÈRE   *Poitou*

Ground Steak Miremonde

Bifteks Miremonde

(Ground beef, bread crumbs, milk, onion, eggs, cream of wheat, nutmeg, wine)

Mix together ¾ pound of ground beef, 2 tablespoons of minced sautéed onion, ¼ cup of bread crumbs moistened with ¼ cup of milk, 2 beaten eggs, 1 tablespoon of cream of wheat, salt, pepper, and a little grated nutmeg. Let the mixture stand for 1 hour, then form it into cakes 1 inch thick. In a covered skillet sauté them slowly in butter, about 10 minutes on each side. Remove them to a hot platter, and add ¼ cup of white wine and 1 tablespoon of chopped parsley to the pan juices. Simmer the sauce, stirring briskly, for a couple of minutes and pour it over the *bifteks* which should be crisp outside and soft and light inside. Serves four.

ROOFTOPS OF PAU   *Béarn*

Chicken Liver and Mushroom Omelette

Omelette Chasseur

(Eggs, chicken livers, mushrooms, shallot, butter, consommé, white wine)

The correct way to fill this classic French omelette is to slit the top of it within a couple of inches of either end after it is folded and turned out on the platter, and then to spread the filling in the slit and sprinkle it with chopped parsley.

Use two small skillets to make the filling. For a 6-egg omelette sauté in the first skillet 3 thinly sliced mushrooms in 1 teaspoon of butter for 4 or 5 minutes; in the second one sauté ½ a small shallot, very finely minced, and 2 chicken livers, each cut into about 6 little pieces, in 1 tablespoon of butter for less than a minute. Do not let the livers get hard or the shallot scorched. Season the livers with salt and pepper, sprinkle them with ¼ teaspoon of flour, and add 1 table-spoon each of chicken consommé and dry white wine (or 2 tablespoons of either one). Blend the mixture quickly, add the mushrooms, and keep the filling warm until the omelette is ready. Serves four.

213

AFTERNOON LIGHT—LA BÉNISSONS DIEU *Lyonnais*

Rolled Shoulder of Lamb Boulangère

Epaule de Mouton à la Boulangère

(Boned shoulder of lamb, butter, onions, potatoes, meat glaze, parsley)

Sprinkle the inside of a boned shoulder of lamb lightly with salt and pepper, roll it tightly and tie it. Melt 4 tablespoons of butter in a small roasting pan, put in the rolled lamb and roast it, uncovered, in a 300° oven, allowing 20 minutes per pound. Baste it with the pan juices and turn it often to brown it evenly. Meanwhile, in a skillet, sauté 20 tiny whole onions, or 5 medium ones, sliced or quartered, in 3 tablespoons of butter until they are golden. Add 5 medium potatoes, cut in pieces, and cook the vegetables together, stirring often, for another 5 minutes. Thirty minutes before the lamb is done, arrange them in the pan around the meat, and roast all together, still basting often. Remove the lamb and vegetables to a hot serving platter. Dissolve 1 teaspoon of meat glaze in ¾ cup of boiling water, stir this into the pan juices, and strain the sauce into a sauce boat. Sprinkle the potatoes and onions with chopped parsley. Serves six.

214

WEST PORTAL, ÉGLISE STE.-FOY—CONQUES *Gascony*

Christmas Eve Smothered Beef

Estouffat de Noël à la Gasconne

(Round of beef, ham rind, spices, herbs, bacon, vegetables, brandy, red wine)

The tradition in Gascony is to cook this savory dish on Christmas Eve and serve it after midnight Mass.

Make 6 small incisions in a 3-pound piece of round of beef and insert half a clove of garlic in each one. In an ovenproof casserole place a piece of ham rind about 4 inches square, add the piece of beef and sprinkle it lightly with salt and pepper and a pinch each of nutmeg and cinnamon. Add a *bouquet garni*, 3 whole cloves, 1 slice of bacon, diced, 4 shallots, cut in halves, 2 medium onions, quartered, and 2 carrots, cut in long strips. Then add ¼ cup of brandy, 2 cups of red wine, ½ cup of beef stock, and enough water almost to cover the meat with liquid. Put a piece of heavy parchment paper over the casserole and tie it tightly around the rim. Put the lid on the casserole and cook the *estouffat* in a 250° oven for about 6 hours. To serve, remove the beef to a deep platter, surround it with the vegetables, and pour the juices over it, first skimming from them as much fat as possible. Serves six.

THE CHÂTEAU OF ST. GERMAIN-EN-LIVET *Normandy*

French Crêpes with Applesauce and Rum
Crêpes Grandgousier
(French crêpes, applesauce, lemon rind, nutmeg, butter, sugar, rum)

This is a delightful variation on the well-known theme of *crêpes Suzette,* and not quite so much trouble:

Make 24 paper-thin French pancakes according to a standard recipe, but flavor them with rum instead of the usual cognac. Season 2½ cups of homemade applesauce with a little grated lemon rind and nutmeg and 2 teaspoons of butter. Simmer it down to thicken into a sort of apple jam. Spread a heaping teaspoon of applesauce in the center of each *crêpe,* roll them all up, arrange them on a buttered heatproof platter and dust them with extra-fine granulated sugar. Put them in a hot oven to glaze for a few minutes. Warm ¼ cup of rum and take it to the table with the platter of *crêpes.* Set a match to the rum, pour it quickly all over the *crêpes,* and serve them on hot plates as soon as the flame dies. Serves six.

216

Menus

❦

HORS-D'OEUVRE VARIES

These are the classic luncheon hors-d'oeuvre. Though elaborate variations are possible, the ones listed below are some of the most usual and they are so rudimentary that actual recipes are given for only seven of them. A balanced selection of three or four items from the total list is quite sufficient for one meal. It is a good cook's pride every now and then, however, to set forth a splendid tray of a dozen or so in matching raviers, *oblong china dishes that are traditional at home as well as in restaurants. It is legitimate, and in fact expected, that the family cook should use her imagination in putting together* hors-d'oeuvre variés *and that she should often use up left-overs in the process. Quantities should be small and French bread and unsalted butter are necessary accompaniments.*

Radishes, eaten with salt, sweet butter, and French bread
Black olives, Greek or Italian type
Vegetable salads, each vegetable in its own dish, with French dressing, minced parsley and/or minced chives or onion. Some possibilities: sliced tomatoes or cucumbers; cooked green beans, white beans, cauliflower, beets or leeks.
Celery root with rémoulade sauce, 156
Cucumbers à la grecque, 49
Onions à la grecque, 78
Mushroom salad, 58
Grilled peppers, 48
Mixed-vegetable salad, cooked, diced, and dressed with mayonnaise

Potato salad
Hard-boiled eggs, halved, with mayonnaise, sometimes garnished with a piece of anchovy
Salami, or any hard sausage of the same type, thinly sliced
Marinated beef, 97
Liver pâté, 22 (or any meat pâté of your choice)
Sardines, with lemon
Canned tuna fish, with lemon, or with mayonnaise and capers
Herring, pickled in oil or white wine
Shrimp, the smaller the better, cooked in a well-seasoned *court-bouillon* (see page 134), chilled, and served with lemon or mayonnaise

LUNCHEONS

Radishes, butter   Tomato salad
Sardines
Omelette with herbs, 61
Cheese
Fruit
Red *or* white wine

Black olives   White bean salad
Salami
Basque omelette, 34
Cheese
Fruit
Red *or* rosé wine

Hors-d'oeuvre variés, 217
Calves' brains with black butter, 90
Steamed potatoes
Spinach purée
Strawberry tart, 7
Red *or* white wine

(Burgundian snails, 147)
Jellied ham with parsley, 122
Salad (chicory)   Cheese
Strawberries with whipped cream, 50
Chablis *or* Meursault Charmes
or California Pinot Blanc

LUNCHEONS or SUPPERS

Cheese tart, 133
Niçoise salad, 55
Fruit
Rosé wine

Riviera pizza, 73
Lobster Alexander, 56
Fruit
White Burgundy
or California Riesling *or* Pinot Blanc

Eggs poached in cream, 113
Braised endive, 126
Swiss cheese
Apples
French butter cookies, 88
White wine

Hot cheese and ham sandwiches, 30
Green salad with fines herbes
Flambéed bananas, 72
Meursault
or California Pinot Chardonnay

SUPPERS

(Onion soup, 17)
Mirasol pork and veal pâté, 128
Green salad (escarole)
Caramel baked pears, 155
Red wine

Pumpkin soup, 102
Stuffed baked tomatoes, 177
Mashed potatoes
Chocolate mousse, 107
White wine

Alsatian ham and beef broth, 186
Ardennes stuffed baked potatoes, 82
Liver pâté, 22   Endive salad
Caramel custard, 51
Beer *or* Alsatian white wine
or California Riesling

Split-pea soup, 108
Burgundian snails, 147
Green salad (lettuce, chicory)
Creamed Camembert, 43
Red Burgundy
or California Cabernet

DINNERS

Consommé
Pheasant with endive, 185
Francine's chocolate cream, 66
Bordeaux *(such as* Léoville-Poyferré)
or California Pinot Noir

Creamed water cress soup, 5
Squab with new peas, 158
Flambéed apricot omelette, 131
Red Bordeaux
or California Pinot Noir

(*Epicures' canapés, 75*)
Fish sauté Romagnole, 193
Steamed potatoes
Baked zucchini,* 110
Fruit

Rosé wine

❧

(*Burgundian snails, 147*)
Chicken in red wine, 21
Steamed potatoes
Salad (garden lettuce)
Cheese (Roquefort)
Hot apple mousse, 179

Red Burgundy
or California Pinot Noir

❧

Burgundian beef stew, with rice, 94
Salad (garden lettuce, water cress)
Cheese (Camembert, Gorgonzola)
Poached peaches, raspberry sauce, 182

Red Burgundy
or California Pinot Noir

❧

(*Leek and potato soup, 54*)
Roast leg of veal with mustard, 136
Buttered noodles
Germaine's creamed spinach,* 63
Hot apple mousse, 179

Red Bordeaux, Arbois, *or* Bourgeuil
or California Cabernet

(*Baked eggs with mushrooms, 44*)
Stuffed shad, 23
New potatoes
Spinach purée
Strawberries and cream, 187

Vouvray *or* Pouilly-Fuissé
or New York State Elvira

❧

(*Stuffed crab Armoricaine, 115*)
Breton roast lamb with white beans, 15
Salad (romaine)
Cheese (Pont l'Evêque, Brie)
Pears amandine, 18

Pouilly-sur-Loire
or California Pinot Blanc

❧

(*Shrimp Nantua, 148*)
Duck with glazed onions, 161
Asparagus, egg and butter sauce,* 199
Fruit

Red Burgundy (*such as* Grands-
Echézeaux) *or* California Cabernet

❧

(*Mushrooms on toast, 208*)
Poached salmon, green mayonnaise, 109
Cucumber-stuffed tomatoes, 109
Cheese (Camembert, Bel Paese)
Grand Marnier soufflé, 166

Meursault *or* Traminer, *or* California
Folle Blanche *or* Pinot Chardonnay

SUNDAY DINNERS

Onions à la grecque, 78
Herring fillets pickled in oil
Cucumber salad   Black olives
Pork tenderloin Lorraine, 27
Brussels sprouts and chestnuts, 28
Green salad (endive, water cress)
Crème brulée, 198

Traminer, Sylvaner, *or* Riesling
or California Riesling

Tomato salad   Liver pâté, 22
Celery root with rémoulade sauce, 156
Radishes, butter   Black olives
Fowl with rice, 47
Braised carrots, 10
Cheese (Port-du-Salut, Camembert)
Francine's apple fritters, 124

Sancerre *or* Pouilly-Fuissé
or California Pinot Chardonnay

* separate course

219

Radishes, butter Salami
Leeks with French dressing
Veal chops en cocotte, 103
Green salad (romaine)
Roquefort Pears

Beaujolais or Côtes du Rhône
or California Pinot Noir

(Eggs in aspic with Madeira, 129)
Black-pepper steak, 130
Green beans with onions, 92
Chestnut pudding, 65

Red Burgundy or Côtes du Rhône
or California Cabernet

Hors-d'oeuvre variés, 217
White wine rabbit stew, 167
Eggplant purée, 146
Cheese (Port-du-Salut, Brie)
Fruit

Arbois or Beaujolais
or California Sauvignon Blanc

(Hot Lorraine tart, 2)
Roast of veal bourgeoise, 117
Cold asparagus salad, French dressing
Puréed apricots and cream, 189

Red Bordeaux
or California Pinot Noir

MIDNIGHT SUPPER

Baked oysters with almonds, 24
Foie gras   Normandy potato salad, 211   Green salad with fines herbes
Flambéed fresh figs, 162
Champagne Demitasse Liqueurs

THANKSGIVING (or Christmas Day)

Oysters on the half shell
Chablis or California Pinot Blanc

Roast turkey, chestnut stuffing, 125
Mashed potatoes French peas, 37
Chambertin or California Cabernet

Endive salad
Assorted cheeses
Upside-down apple tart, 93

Demitasse Liqueurs

CHRISTMAS EVE

Oysters on the half shell
Chablis or California Pinot Chardonnay

Christmas Eve smothered beef, 215
with steamed potatoes
Red Bordeaux or California Pinot Noir
Water cress salad Camembert, 43

Crêpes Grandgousier, 216
Champagne

Demitasse Liqueurs

FORMAL DINNER

Chicken consommé velouté, 192
Scallops Saint-Jacques. 39
Puligny-Montrachet

Avignon flambéed filets mignons, 52
Pommard-Epenots

Foie gras
Garden lettuce salad with fines herbes
Assorted cheeses

Poached peaches, raspberry sauce, 182
Château La Tour Blanche

Demitasse Liqueurs

BANQUET

Cold Madrilène consommé, 140
Trout with almonds and cream, 57
Alsatian Gewürztraminer

Roast tenderloin of beef jardinière, 86
Musigny (also with next course)

Guinea hen chasseur, 173
Water cress and lettuce salad
Assorted cheeses

Coupe Jacques, 169
Champagne

Demitasse Petits fours Liqueurs

Menu Planner

The bilingual recipe index which follows is designed to serve as a menu planner as well as to locate recipes by name. The English entries, therefore, include the following categories:

Recipe Index

223

229

231